Oil

Other Books in the Current Controversies Series

Biodiversity

Blogs

Capital Punishment

Darfur

Disaster Response

Drug Trafficking

Espionage and Intelligence

Food

Global Warming

Human Trafficking

Immigration

Online Social Networking

Poverty and Homelessness

Prisons

Racism

Resistant Infections

The U.S. Economy

The World Economy

Violence Against Women

Oil

Debra A. Miller, Book Editor

GREENHAVEN PRESS
A part of Gale, Cengage Learning

Detroit • New York • San Francisco • New Haven, Conn • Waterville, Maine • London

GALE
CENGAGE Learning™

Christine Nasso, *Publisher*
Elizabeth Des Chenes, *Managing Editor*

© 2010 Greenhaven Press, a part of Gale, Cengage Learning

Gale and Greenhaven Press are registered trademarks used herein under license.

For more information, contact:
Greenhaven Press
27500 Drake Rd.
Farmington Hills, MI 48331-3535
Or you can visit our Internet site at gale.cengage.com

LIBRARY OF CONGRESS CATALOGING-IN-PUBLICATION DATA

Oil / Debra A. Miller, book editor.
   p. cm. -- (Current controversies)
  Includes bibliographical references and index.
  ISBN 978-0-7377-4919-9 (hbk.) -- ISBN 978-0-7377-4920-5 (pbk.)
  1. Petroleum reserves--Juvenile literature. 2. Petroleum industry and trade--Juvenile literature. 3. Energy consumption--Juvenile literature. I. I. Miller, Debra A.
  HD9565.O553 2010
  333.8'232--dc22

                                   2009051886

Printed in the United States of America
1 2 3 4 5 6 7 14 13 12 11 10

Contents

Foreword   **13**

Introduction   **16**

Chapter 1: Is the World Benefiting from Oil?

Chapter Overview   **21**

Gal Luft

For 150 years, oil has brought global economic growth and prosperity; it also has caused international conflict and political volatility. Today rising oil prices and dependence on oil as the main transportation fuel are proving to be a toxic combination, but the development of new transportation technologies still faces many challenges.

Yes: The World Is Benefiting from Oil

Oil Has Brought Astounding Benefits   **31**
to Human Civilization

Environmental Literacy Council

Oil is a miracle resource—both cheap and highly efficient—and it has fueled a wave of human prosperity over the last hundred years, providing benefits such as enhanced mobility, affordable consumer products, widespread access to air travel, and health care advances. Although oil use does negatively impact the environment, it will continue to be a major source of energy.

Oil Is Vital to the World Economy   **34**

Terry Hathaway

Ever since the automobile became the main mode of transportation, oil has been vitally important to the world economy. Today the world consumes more than 85 million barrels of crude oil—refined into gasoline, jet fuel, and diesel—daily. Global oil consumption is expected to grow in the future, due largely to economic development in China and India.

The Oil and Natural Gas Industry Is   37
an Essential Part of the U.S. Economy
   Myra Crownover

The drilling practices in Texas offer an example of the
economic benefits the oil and natural gas industry provides for the United States. The industry is one of the
largest employers in the country and provides numerous
benefits for the overall economy.

No: The World Is Not Benefiting from Oil

America's Dependence on Middle Eastern   41
Oil Was the Reason for the Iraq War
   James Cogan

Contrary to claims about terrorism and weapons of mass
destruction, the true objectives of the six-year-long war
in Iraq were to achieve military domination of the Persian Gulf region and gain access and control of Iraqi oil.
The Barack Obama administration is continuing the occupation for the same reasons.

Oil Wealth Fuels Conflict Within   46
Oil-Producing Countries
   Michael L. Ross

Oil brought great wealth to many petroleum-rich, developing countries. For many, however, this blessing became
a curse, as volatile oil markets and ineffective governance
often resulted in debt, corruption, high unemployment,
and sluggish or declining economies. Oil wealth also has
contributed to numerous armed conflicts and civil wars.

Oil Wealth Sustains Oil Tyrannies   56
Around the World
   Alvaro Vargas Llosa

Oil profits have created and are sustaining dictatorships
in many oil-producing countries, providing dictators
with cash that can be used as bribes, to stifle dissent, and
in some cases, to obtain the cooperation of neighboring
states. Many of these regimes, through incompetence and
corruption, have caused shortages in world oil supplies,
and then they reap the benefits of higher oil prices.

Chapter 2: How Has the World's Reliance on Oil Affected the Environment?

Chapter Preface   **60**

A Century of Oil Has Taken a Heavy   **63**
Toll on the Environment

Union of Concerned Scientists

Oil drilling and transport have caused serious damage to the environment throughout the twentieth century. Oil extraction can cause soil and groundwater contamination, and oil spills can cause ecological disasters to our oceans and waterways. Air pollution from cars and other transportation is even worse, releasing toxic gases and particulates that contribute to urban smog, acid rain, and global warming; causing health problems in humans and animals; and damaging crops, forests, and habitat.

Oil Spills and Leaks Cause   **73**
Environmental Disasters

Greenpeace

Marine ecosystems already stressed by overfishing, toxic pollution, and climate change are suffering from daily oil spills, both large and small. These spills smother marine life by coating feathers and fur and poison birds, mammals, and fish. Oil spills can also cause nausea and health problems for people in affected areas and can have long-lasting negative environmental effects.

Oil and Gas Drilling Operations Have   **79**
Degraded the Environment of the Western
United States

Dusty Horwitt

Oil and natural gas operations have drilled thousands of wells on pristine lands in the western part of the United States, causing serious environmental degradation. Since 2000, drilling has intensified, largely because oil companies are exempted from most major federal environmental laws.

Oil Extraction Threatens the Amazon   **83**
Rain Forests

   Rhett Butler

   Oil production has caused the deforestation, degradation, and destruction of lands around the world. Today it is destroying parts of precious tropical rain forests. Drilling releases toxic by-products into local rivers; broken pipelines and leaks result in destructive oil spills; and the construction of roads to reach remote tropical oil sites opens these lands to settlers and land developers.

Increasing Demand for Fossil Fuels Will   **88**
Cause Even Greater Environmental Damage
in the Future

   Agence France-Presse (AFP)

   According to the International Energy Agency (IEA), the demand for fossil fuels will likely explode over the next two decades, largely due to rapid economic development in China and India. This trend projects that unless a technological transformation on a massive scale occurs, greenhouse gas emissions will increase instead of decrease, adding to global warming.

Peak Oil Could Have Disastrous Effects on   **92**
the Environment

   Grinning Planet

   Peak oil will probably have a devastating impact on the environment, because oil companies will seek to extract oil from non-conventional sources (such as Canadian tar sands) and from deep ocean waters, which pose greater environmental challenges. In addition, the world will no doubt turn to other environmentally destructive energy sources such as coal, biofuel, and nuclear energy.

**Chapter 3: Is the World Running
Out of Oil?**

Chapter Preface   **104**

Yes: The World Is Running Out of Oil

The World Oil Supply Is Running Out Fast   **107**

Steve Connor

A study of the world's oil fields has concluded that most of the biggest fields have already peaked and that oil production is now declining almost twice as rapidly as just two years ago. In addition, many oil-producing countries are not investing in new oil developments. This could result in a major energy crunch within the next five years, which could cripple global economic recovery.

Peak Oil Occurred on a Worldwide   **113**
Basis in 2008

Richard Heinberg

Many analysts believe that peak oil took place on a worldwide basis early in 2008, and it may be useful to remember July 11, 2008, as Peak Oil Day, because on that day oil prices reached their high-water mark. In the future, although temporary rises in production may occur, the oil supply will continue to decline.

The U.S. Government Predicts a Sharp   **116**
Drop in World Oil Output

Michael T. Klare

The *International Energy Outlook 2009* predicts a sharp drop in future world oil output along with an increased reliance on unconventional fuels such as oil sands, ultra-deep oil, shale oil, and biofuels. This is an admission from DOE that global fuel supplies will not be sufficient to meet rising world energy demands.

No: The World Is Not Running Out of Oil

Peak Oil Is a Myth   **125**

Jason Schwarz

The facts do not support the peak oil theory because high oil prices have enabled oil companies to expand exploration and development, allowing them to locate numerous new sources of oil. Among them are several deep ocean fields, new reserves in Iraq and Iran, and large shale oil resources in the United States and Canada.

Oil Will Be a Growth Business for
the Next Twenty Years

129

Daniel Yergin

Recent studies show that ample oil resources exist underground, but factors such as oil price volatility, concerns about global warming, and globalized demand should drive governments to fund research of technological solutions to world energy problems. Whatever the technological breakthroughs, however, economic growth in the developing world will make oil a global growth business for years to come.

Humans Will Find a Better Energy Source
Long Before Oil Runs Out

133

Brian Dunning

Oil is a finite resource, therefore global peak oil will occur at some point, especially if China and India continue to grow economically, increasing demand. Significant research is already under way to develop alternative fuel vehicles and alternatives to other petroleum-based products, however, and by the time oil runs out, scientists will likely have developed a solution.

Chapter 4: How Does Oil Affect the Future?

Chapter Preface

140

Oil Will Continue to Impact
the Global Economy

144

Michael T. Klare

Although renewable energy sources will no doubt be increasingly important to the global energy market, oil will continue to be the dominant form of energy for at least the next several decades. In the future, oil prices are likely to rise again, but whether prices are high or low, the world cannot escape the difficult consequences of its dependence on oil.

Rising Oil Prices May Threaten   153
Oil Production and Supply
  Greenpeace

    The depletion of easy-to-access oil and fluctuations in
    the price of oil present significant challenges for interna-
    tional oil companies that hope to develop more expen-
    sive oil resources, such as tar sand projects, deep-water
    oil fields, and offshore Arctic oil resources. The expense
    of bringing this new oil to market requires high oil prices,
    but if prices rise too high, demand for oil could decrease,
    which could slow production and reduce supply.

Higher Oil Prices Could Strain Global   162
Agriculture Systems
  Jason Mark

    Both U.S. and global food production systems are com-
    pletely dependent on oil, which produces the synthetic
    nitrogen fertilizers essential for high crop yields, the
    gasoline and diesel fuels that power farm equipment and
    ship foods around the globe, and the electricity needed
    to run processing factories. If global oil prices rise sig-
    nificantly or if oil production drops, the world food sys-
    tem will be strained, threatening our ability to feed our-
    selves.

The Security of Oil Supply and Demand Is   170
Necessary to Sustain the Global Economy
  Ali Hussain

    Because of the importance of oil, maintaining security of
    oil supplies is one of the most important concerns for
    oil-consuming countries, just as maintaining stable de-
    mand is important to oil-producing countries.

The United States Must Unleash   180
a New Clean Energy Economy
  Barack Obama

    The U.S. dependence on oil comes at a high cost to the
    economy and the environment, and the nation must lay
    a new foundation for economic growth by beginning a
    new era of energy exploration in America. The United
    States must be the nation that leads the world in creating
    new clean energy sources—it's a choice between our pros-
    perity and our decline.

Sustainability Is the Next Phase   **191**
of Human Development
    Eric McLamb
    The Industrial Revolution dramatically changed every as-
    pect of human life, but the impact of these human ac-
    tivities on the environment, public health, energy usage,
    and sanitation did not become clear until some two hun-
    dred years after its beginnings. Changing an energy sys-
    tem that is so interwoven into our economy will take
    time and resources, but it will happen, and the world
    will enter a new era of sustainability.

Organizations to Contact   **195**

Bibliography   **201**

Index   **207**

Foreword

By definition, controversies are "discussions of questions in which opposing opinions clash" (Webster's Twentieth Century Dictionary Unabridged). Few would deny that controversies are a pervasive part of the human condition and exist on virtually every level of human enterprise. Controversies transpire between individuals and among groups, within nations and between nations. Controversies supply the grist necessary for progress by providing challenges and challengers to the status quo. They also create atmospheres where strife and warfare can flourish. A world without controversies would be a peaceful world; but it also would be, by and large, static and prosaic.

The Series' Purpose

The purpose of the Current Controversies series is to explore many of the social, political, and economic controversies dominating the national and international scenes today. Titles selected for inclusion in the series are highly focused and specific. For example, from the larger category of criminal justice, Current Controversies deals with specific topics such as police brutality, gun control, white collar crime, and others. The debates in Current Controversies also are presented in a useful, timeless fashion. Articles and book excerpts included in each title are selected if they contribute valuable, long-range ideas to the overall debate. And wherever possible, current information is enhanced with historical documents and other relevant materials. Thus, while individual titles are current in focus, every effort is made to ensure that they will not become quickly outdated. Books in the Current Controversies series will remain important resources for librarians, teachers, and students for many years.

In addition to keeping the titles focused and specific, great care is taken in the editorial format of each book in the series. Book introductions and chapter prefaces are offered to provide background material for readers. Chapters are organized around several key questions that are answered with diverse opinions representing all points on the political spectrum. Materials in each chapter include opinions in which authors clearly disagree as well as alternative opinions in which authors may agree on a broader issue but disagree on the possible solutions. In this way, the content of each volume in Current Controversies mirrors the mosaic of opinions encountered in society. Readers will quickly realize that there are many viable answers to these complex issues. By questioning each author's conclusions, students and casual readers can begin to develop the critical thinking skills so important to evaluating opinionated material.

Current Controversies is also ideal for controlled research. Each anthology in the series is composed of primary sources taken from a wide gamut of informational categories including periodicals, newspapers, books, U.S. and foreign government documents, and the publications of private and public organizations. Readers will find factual support for reports, debates, and research papers covering all areas of important issues. In addition, an annotated table of contents, an index, a book and periodical bibliography, and a list of organizations to contact are included in each book to expedite further research.

Perhaps more than ever before in history, people are confronted with diverse and contradictory information. During the Persian Gulf War, for example, the public was not only treated to minute-to-minute coverage of the war, it was also inundated with critiques of the coverage and countless analyses of the factors motivating U.S. involvement. Being able to sort through the plethora of opinions accompanying today's major issues, and to draw one's own conclusions, can be a complicated and frustrating struggle. It is the editors' hope that Current Controversies will help readers with this struggle.

Introduction

"The modern age of oil ... did not begin until the latter 1800s, after the first oil well was drilled in the United States and the internal combustion engine was invented and developed to run on gasoline, one of the products of crude oil."

Oil, a resource that took the earth millions of years to create, is rapidly being consumed by modern humans. Oil is a fossil fuel, which means that it formed more than 300 million years ago when small sea creatures (such as algae and plankton) died, fell to the ocean floor, and were buried under sediment and rock until the pressure and heat turned them into oil. As the earth's surface moved and buckled over many centuries, oil migrated into underground pockets, trapped between layers of rock. Early humans used oil that seeped to the surface for various purposes—as medicine, to waterproof canoes, and in the construction of buildings and roads. The modern age of oil, however, did not begin until the latter 1800s, after the first oil well was drilled in the United States and the internal combustion engine was invented and developed to run on gasoline, one of the products of crude oil. The direct result of those discoveries is a world addicted to oil. Today most of the developed world relies on cheap oil to power the world economy—mostly as a transportation fuel, but also for a variety of other purposes.

Today's oil era began just 150 years ago in the small community of Titusville in northwestern Pennsylvania. On August 27, 1859, a former railroad worker named Edwin L. Drake, also known as Colonel Drake, used a steam engine to drill for oil in an underground well and pumped it to the surface. Drake's success was the result of several years' research by a

New York lawyer, George Bissell, who noticed that a dark, oily substance was present in the ground in that region of Pennsylvania. Bissell had the substance tested by scientists and found that it could be processed into a fluid for lighting lamps and used as a lubricant for machines. The prospect of finding a source of inexpensive lamp oil was very exciting because at the time most people used either simple candles or whale oil for lighting, and overfishing of whales had led to a decline in the whale population and a dramatic increase in whale oil prices. The next step, after finding investors, was to determine if the oil could be produced in a sufficient quantity to make it commercially viable. With this goal in mind, Bissell employed Drake and charged him with obtaining the mineral rights in the Titusville area and conducting a search for oil.

Drake's first well hit oil after drilling for sixty-nine feet and eventually yielded about a thousand barrels of oil a day for three years. This initial discovery launched an oil rush that attracted speculators from around the country in search of "Black Gold." Later, much larger deposits of oil were discovered in Texas. A new industry—the refining of oil for kerosene fuel for use in lamps—developed, and over the years the industry became monopolized by John D. Rockefeller, owner of the Standard Oil Company (later broken up into several companies, including today's Exxon corporation).

In the early 1900s, oil became important to another industry when American entrepreneur Henry Ford founded an automobile company to manufacture cars with internal combustion engines that could run on gasoline, once considered a waste product created during the refining of oil for kerosene. Ford launched the mass-produced Model T car in 1908, giving Americans an affordable vehicle and making the internal combustion vehicle the standard car design. Other forms of oil-powered transportation followed, including trucks, airplanes, and boats that run on gasoline or other types of oil-based fuels, such as diesel and jet fuel. By the 1950s, electricity had replaced kerosene lamps and oil was mostly used as a fuel for transportation. Today, two-thirds of the world's oil supply is used for transportation with the remaining third used for heating, road surfacing, and electricity generation and as an essential ingredient for the manufacture of plastics, lubricants, fertilizers and pesticides, and countless other goods and necessities.

After it founded the oil age, the United States dominated world oil production throughout the early twentieth century. U.S. fields produced more than 70 percent of world oil production in 1925, about 63 percent in 1941, and more than 50 percent in 1950. In addition, five of the world's seven largest oil companies were American companies that held oil interests around the globe. U.S. oil companies, for example, obtained holdings in two Latin American countries where oil was discovered—Mexico and Venezuela—and in the 1920s and early 1930s acquired oil concessions in the oil-rich Middle East. By the beginning of World War II, in addition to marketing the oil from wells in America, U.S. companies produced almost 40 percent of oil found outside the United States and the Soviet Union.

By the 1970s, however, U.S. oil production began to decline. Although no one could believe it at the time, a prediction made in 1956 by Shell geoscientist M. King Hubbert proved true—that U.S. petroleum production would peak between the late 1960s and early 1970s and then begin a rapid decline. The Middle East now holds the world's largest deposits of oil, although oil fields have also been discovered in many other countries. In 1960 the Organization of the Petroleum Exporting Countries (OPEC) was formed by a number of Middle Eastern oil producers to control oil production and pricing. Today OPEC members control about 40 percent of global crude oil production and about 77 percent of the world's crude oil reserves, giving them the ability to cut back on world oil supply whenever necessary to keep oil prices and profits high.

Many energy experts believe that global oil supplies are now peaking, just as U.S. oil production did in the 1970s. The world currently uses about 85 million barrels of oil per day—a level that is becoming increasingly difficult for producers to maintain. Experts explain that although oil is still plentiful on the planet, much of the oil that is easy to find has already been tapped, leaving only oil deposits that are more difficult and more expensive to develop. In recent years, with developing countries such as India and China increasing their oil usage, oil producers appeared unable to increase the global oil supply enough to satisfy demand, and this helped rocket oil prices to a peak of $147 per barrel in 2008. Many observers credit this spike in oil prices as a trigger for a recession that subsequently gripped much of the world. The recession, in turn, caused demand for oil to fall along with oil prices. Numerous forecasts predict, however, that another oil supply shortage is in the near future, as economies recover and developing countries continue their explosive economic growth.

Policy makers around the world are now studying how to transition their economies from oil to other types of fuel, not only because oil may be running out, but also because oil has caused so many serious environmental problems, the most significant of which is global warming. So far, however, despite experimentation with new green energy sources such as solar, wind, and geothermal energy, no real substitute for oil has been found yet. To some observers, the world appears to be entering a period of volatility, in which countries may compete (or even fight) for dwindling resources, and the world economy is challenged to absorb shocks from changing prices of oil and other commodities.

The authors of the viewpoints included in *Current Controversies: Oil* elaborate on various aspects of this oil story, including whether oil resources have benefited or harmed the world, how oil has affected the environment, whether oil is really running out, and what the future holds for both producers and consumers of oil.

Is the World Benefiting from Oil?

Chapter Overview

Gal Luft

Gal Luft is executive director of the Institute for the Analysis of Global Security (IAGS) and publisher of the Journal of Energy Security. *He is also a coeditor of the book* Energy Security Challenges for the 21st Century.

One hundred and fifty years ago, on August 27, 1859, Colonel Edwin Drake struck oil in Titusville, Pennsylvania, giving rise to the modern oil industry. What was sought as a replacement for depleting stocks of whale oil used as a fuel for lamps, gradually turned into the world's most strategic commodity. Today oil supplies 40% of global energy.

A Source of Property and Volatility

During its century-and-a-half-long history, oil has been a source of both prosperity and global volatility. Petroleum has enabled the production of industrial chemicals, heating oil, medicines, plastics, asphalt and lubricants, all of them critical to our modern society. (Contrary to popular belief, the US [United States] uses very little oil today to make electricity. At present, only 2% of US electricity is generated from oil.) Most importantly, oil has enabled mobility, and hence a rapid flow of goods and services, perhaps the key contributing factor to the impressive global economic growth of the 20th century. Today, roughly two-thirds of the world's oil is used for transportation. Petroleum enjoys a near monopoly in this sector—most of the world's cars, trucks, planes, ships and trains are able to run on nothing but it.

On the other side of the balance sheet, global economic dependence on oil and its products has bred considerable trouble. Oil [has] become a backdrop behind great powers' foreign policies and has been a driver of some of the past century's most seminal events. Imperial Japan's insatiable need for oil led it to adopt in the 1930s an expansionist policy that triggered an oil embargo by the US, then supplier of 80% of the island's oil imports. Tokyo's response, sending its navy to attack Pearl Harbor, provoked a four-year war in the Pacific which took two mushroom clouds to end. In Europe, Nazi Germany's need for oil compelled Adolf Hitler to invade Russia and later to divert his panzers from Moscow to the Soviet oil center in Baku, a decision that sealed the fate of the Third Reich.

During its century-and-a-half-long history, oil has been a source of both prosperity and global volatility.

With the war's end, attention shifted to the Middle East as the world's most important source of oil and the key to the stability of the global economy. Today, this tumultuous region produces nearly 40% of the world's oil and is home to two-thirds of proven global conventional oil reserves and to over half of undiscovered reserves. Since the historic February 1945 meeting aboard the USS *Quincy* between the ailing US President Franklin D. Roosevelt and King Abdul Aziz ibn Saud of Saudi Arabia, oil considerations have governed US Middle East policy, and the US has considered it essential to engage in military activity in order to ensure continued access to the Persian Gulf. The Carter Doctrine, the "reflagging" of Kuwaiti tankers during the Iran-Iraq War, the 1991 Gulf War and US military presence in Saudi Arabia, Qatar, Bahrain, Kuwait and, most recently, Iraq, have all been tied to America's energy security needs.

The Cost of US Oil Dependence

For the US, the dependence on oil comes at a cost. It has forced Washington to establish "special relations" with nondemocratic and unpopular regimes, such as those of the Shah of Iran and the House of Saud, while US military presence in the region has been a lightning rod for the region's radicals. In February 2005, President George W. Bush conceded that "the policy in the past used to be, let's just accept tyranny, for the sake of [...] cheap oil [...] and just hope everything would be okay. Well, that changed on September the 11th [2001, when terrorists attacked America]. Everything wasn't okay. Beneath what appeared to be a placid surface lurked an ideology based upon hatred." Also on the negative side: The global oil industry is more than ever a government-dominated business. More than 80% of the world's reserves are controlled by governments and their proxies, and what was once the privately owned Seven Sisters [seven oil companies that provided much of the oil production, refining, and distribution during the mid-twentieth century] are now seven midgets in comparison to the 'new Seven Sisters,' all government run: Saudi Aramco, Russia's Gazprom, China's CNPC [China National Petroleum Corporation], Iran's NIOC [National Iranian Oil Corporation], Venezuela's PDVSA [Petróleos de Venezuela, S.A.], Brazil's Petrobras and Malaysia's Petronas. Such government control over the world's fuel supply makes oil a tool of foreign policy which was clearly demonstrated during the 1973 Arab oil embargo.

> *Oil [has] become a backdrop behind great powers' foreign policies and has been a driver of some of the past century's most seminal events.*

A world of high oil prices is a poison pill for everything the US and its allies are trying to accomplish abroad from democracy promotion and human rights protection to counterproliferation of terrorism and nuclear weapons. With few exceptions, oil-exporting countries' human rights records leave much to be desired. Only 10% of the world's proven reserves are concentrated in countries ranked "free" by Freedom House. In many countries highly dependent on oil revenues for their income, such as Sudan, Azerbaijan, Kazakhstan, Saudi Arabia, Iran, Angola, Nigeria, Chad, Venezuela and Russia, high oil prices enable authoritarian regimes to consolidate their power and erode progress toward freedom and democracy. As a result, in many parts of the world, millions of people have been enslaved, oppressed and denied basic freedoms by nondemocratic oil regimes aided by the silence of the importers who depend upon them. Then Secretary of State Condoleezza Rice in 2006 offered senators telling testimony revealing the depth of frustration with the toxic influence oil dependence has on America's foreign policy: "Nothing has really taken me aback more, as secretary of state, than the way that the politics of energy is [. . .] 'warping' diplomacy around the world."

Oil considerations have governed US Middle East policy, and the US has considered it essential to engage in military activity in order to ensure continued access to the Persian Gulf.

Redefining Energy Independence

The array of security, economic and environmental challenges associated with US oil dependence have popularized the call for "energy independence" beyond any other issue in America's political discourse. Public opinion polls show that Americans, regardless of their political affiliation, see energy independence as an urgent imperative. President Barack Obama's first budget proposal was tied to a renewable energy program "to help the US move toward energy independence." Yet, despite its popular appeal, in many circles the concept is met with skepticism—in some cases outright contempt. Energy independence has been referred to as a "pipe dream," a "misguided quest" and a "dangerous illusion." A Council on Foreign Relations task force went so far as to accuse those promoting energy independence of "doing the nation a disservice." The critics' skepticism stems from their literal interpretation of the concept: They view "independence" as self-sufficiency, or not importing oil even though the US remains dependent on it. Under this interpretation, energy independence is indeed unattainable. The US consumes about 21 million barrels per day, 60% of which are imported. If these barrels were attached to each other they would make a pipe long enough to connect New York and Beijing. For a country that owns barely 3% of the world's conventional oil reserves, replacing such a vast amount of oil with domestic resources is mission impossible.

A world of high oil prices is a poison pill for everything the US and its allies are trying to accomplish abroad.

But self-sufficiency is not what independence means. The problem of oil dependence is not about the amount of oil consumed or imported. The problem is that oil is a strategic commodity by virtue of its virtual monopoly over transportation fuel. This monopoly gives a small group of nations inordinate power on the world's stage. "Independence," as Webster's dictionary says, is "not being subject to control by others," or in our case, being a free actor by reducing the role of oil in world politics—turning it from a strategic commodity into one interchangeable with others.

This is exactly what happened to another commodity which was once monopolized, and considered critical to humanity's functioning: salt. Odd as it seems, for centuries salt mines conferred national power. Wars were fought over salt. Colonies were formed in remote places where it happened to be found. That was because salt had a virtual monopoly over food preservation. With the advent of canning, electricity, and refrigeration, salt lost its strategic status, and salt-rich domains like Orissa, Tortuga and Boa Vista that once held as much sway as today's Gulf Emirates are no longer places of strategic importance. Countries still use, import, and trade salt, but salt is no longer a commodity that dictates world affairs. Turning oil into salt is what energy independence is all about.

The world may no longer be awash with conventional oil, but the amount of reserves offshore and in . . . non-conventional sources . . . can extend oil's play for many years to come.

When in a Hole, Stop Digging

Oil's monopoly over transportation fuel is complicated by the fact that this monopoly is also married to a cartel. During the past four decades, members of the Organization of [the] Petroleum Exporting Countries (OPEC), which collectively sit atop 78% of world oil reserves, have been producing far less than their geological endowment permits. In 1973, just before the Arab oil embargo, OPEC produced 30 million barrels per day. Thirty-six years later, with global demand and non-OPEC production having nearly doubled, and despite the fact that in 2007 the cartel swallowed two new members—Angola and Ecuador—with combined daily production capacity equivalent to that of Norway, OPEC's crude production has not increased. In fact, in 2009 it is expected to average 29 million barrels a day—less than in 1973.

For OPEC, oil's 150th anniversary is a somber one. It comes at a time of deep global recession which has shaved $100 per barrel off the historically high price oil hit last summer. Persian Gulf economies have been dealt painful blows by oil output cuts, heavy losses in their sovereign wealth funds and weak consumer demand. The cartel's revenues in 2009 are projected to fall by more than 60% from last year's one trillion dollar income. If the recession is prolonged, we could see

the first signs of social discontent leading to political rever-
berations in petrodollar-dependent economies. Adding to the
producers' angst are the repeated calls for energy independence coming from Washington's political class and the
[Barack] Obama administration's signals that the US would be
part of a post-Kyoto climate agreement which would impose
an additional cost on use of hydrocarbons. This leaves little
appetite among producers to invest the billions of dollars necessary to prepare the oil industry for the post-recession era.
The International Energy Agency (IEA) recently concluded
that even with the current recession, by 2030 global demand
for oil could increase by 25%. At the same time, the agency
examined the status of the world's 800 top oil fields and reported an average annual depletion rate of 5.5% increasing to
8.6% in 2030. In order to meet future projected demand for
oil, four new Saudi Arabias will have to be added to the global
oil market between now and 2030. But the current economic
conditions have thwarted the much-needed investment in new
production. According to OPEC, since last year, 35 major exploration projects have been shelved. Ali Al-Naimi, the Saudi
oil minister, during the March OPEC meeting, warned of a
coming "catastrophic" shortfall in petroleum production, raising doubts the world can count on the one Saudi Arabia that
exists, not the least on the four that don't. Failure by producers to prepare the ground for the post-recession era could
cause a severe oil-price shock reminiscent of that in 2008 once
the economy recovers and demand for liquid fuels surges.
This could, in turn, send the world into a new round of economic turmoil, leading to a W-shaped, double-dipped recovery instead of a traditional V-shaped recovery in which economic growth bounces back quickly from a slump. And yet,
despite the geological, strategic, economic, and environmental
indicators showing that in the coming decades the cost of
maintaining the oil economy will grow exponentially, we ignore the dictum "when in a hole, stop digging": Every year

more than 50 million new petroleum-only cars roll onto the planet's roads, each with an average street life of 15 years, hence locking humanity's future to petroleum-exporting nations and their whims for many years to come. The recent introduction of the $2,000 Tata Nano, the world's cheapest car, which aims to fulfill the aspirations for fast mobility of hundreds of millions of potential motorists in the developing world, is the latest manifestation of the mismatch between the growing number of gasoline-only vehicle platforms produced worldwide and the ability of the oil industry to power them.

As importers chart their way away from oil, they will likely discover that along with . . . such a shift come new challenges of growing dependence on alternative commodities.

From Monopoly to Fuel Choice

Addressing the energy security challenge requires an understanding that much-touted policies that aim to either increase oil supply through domestic drilling or the ones that decrease its use by boosting fuel efficiency, while helpful, are insufficient as they ignore the main enabler of the oil monopoly: the petroleum-only vehicle. In fact, experience of the past three decades shows that whenever non-OPEC producers increase their production, OPEC decreases supply accordingly. Similarly, when demand for oil drops OPEC quickly responds with production cuts. In other words, when we drill more, OPEC drills less; when we use less, OPEC drills less. Changing this vexing dynamic requires competition and fuel choice in the transportation sector which can only be achieved if new vehicles are built as platforms on which fuels can compete.

A few types of vehicle technologies already offer such a possibility. The first, and most affordable, is the flex-fuel vehicle that can run on any combination of gasoline and alcohol

(alcohol does not mean just ethanol, and ethanol does not mean just corn). The technology is a century old. Henry Ford's Model T was a flex-fuel vehicle. It costs an extra $100 per new car to make a regular car flex-fuel. All it takes is a fuel sensor and a corrosion-resistant fuel line, since alcohol is more corrosive than gasoline. . . .

A Looming Face-Off

The pace of market diffusion of new transportation technologies leaves no doubt that in the coming years the transportation sector will become decreasingly captive to oil. Petroleum-exporting countries wishing to prolong the economic system on which they thrive will be forced to fight for their market share in the face of deepening cracks in their strategic dominance. But for all its challenges, oil is not likely to easily vacate its pedestal, and the arrows in the quiver of its producers are still many.

The world may no longer be awash with conventional oil, but the amount of reserves offshore and in the universe of non-conventional sources like oil shale and tar sands, can extend oil's play for many years to come, albeit at potentially high environmental cost. Producers will have to do more to flatten the roller coaster of oil prices seen in recent months mainly through closer coordination between OPEC and Russia, mothballing (preparing oil fields for recovery but not touching them unless there is clear demand) and by increasing spare production capacity. Their fortunes will be bolstered by non-trivial and often unexpected challenges alternative fuels and advanced automotive technologies will face on their way to mass market penetration. . . .

As importers chart their way away from oil, they will likely discover that along with the geopolitical benefits associated with such a shift come new challenges of growing dependence on alternative commodities. While Asia controls the market for advanced batteries, South America is the source of the materials from which batteries are made. More than 80% of the world's reserve base of lithium is concentrated in South America. Bolivia, a drug-producing country that last year expelled the US ambassador, owns nearly half of the world's economically recoverable lithium. Shifting the epicenter of the world's energy system from the Persian Gulf to East Asia and South America will over time recalibrate nations' foreign policies, reshuffle political alliances and create new strategic interests as was the case in previous centuries when humanity traded one dependence with another. Whether or not this new energy landscape will improve America's posture abroad is premature to determine. But from today's vantage point—heading toward a situation in which, in the words of the chief economist of the IEA, "95% of the world relying for its economic well-being on decisions made by five or six countries in the Middle East"—such over-the-horizon risk seems worth taking. The prospects of a nuclear Middle East, with massive youth bulges, lurking social discontent and persistent oppression, holding the key to global mobility should be enough of an impetus to ensure that on its 200th anniversary oil be no more central to the world economy than salt is today.

Oil Has Brought Astounding Benefits to Human Civilization

Environmental Literacy Council

The Environmental Literacy Council is an independent organization that helps teachers, students, policy makers, and the public find cross-disciplinary resources on the environment.

The twentieth century has been called the "hydrocarbon century." Over the last one hundred years human society has experienced more change than was seen in the previous ten thousand years, in large part because of the availability of a relatively cheap and highly efficient supply of energy: petroleum.

Benefits of Oil

Petroleum has brought enumerable benefits to human civilization; quality of life and dynamic prosperity [are] fueled by this precious, miraculous resource. At the beginning of the twentieth century, global oil output was about 150 million barrels of oil; today, that amount is extracted globally in just two days. Petroleum-based technologies have transformed the global economy, providing mobility unimaginable to previous generations. The rise of the automobile, the manufacture and distribution of affordable consumer products, mass access to air travel, and advances in health care—doubling the average life expectancy in just 100 years—are just a few of the many benefits petroleum has helped bring developed society.

Environmental Literacy Council, "Petroleum," April 21, 2008. www.enviroliteracy.org. © 2002 The Environmental Literacy Council. All rights reserved. Reproduced by permission.

The U.S. [United States] is the world's largest consumer of oil, accounting for nearly 25 percent of global consumption in 2006, followed by the European Union with 18 percent. During this same time, countries within the Middle East produced 31.2 percent of the world's supply of oil. Also, with respect to proven reserves, Middle Eastern nations held 61.5 percent; Russia and Venezuela each held over 6.6 percent; Africa held 9.7 percent; and North America accounted for 5 percent.

Petroleum has brought enumerable benefits to human civilization; quality of life and dynamic prosperity [are] fueled by this precious, miraculous resource.

Environmental Costs and the Future

While the benefits are astounding, the use of petroleum-based technologies also has costs. Perhaps the most serious stems from the emission of greenhouse gases and their contribution to global climate change. And, though there are alternatives to petroleum fuels being proposed for that very reason, an analysis of costs and benefits shows that petroleum is superior in most areas.

Hydrogen, ethanol, hybrid, and biomass technologies are promising substitutes which may increase efficiency and reduce emissions, but these technologies are only beginning to prove their profitability to providers or attractiveness to consumers. Yet, the sustainability of ethanol is now being questioned due to the land and water requirements to grow the corn crop, the effect of using fossil fuels to process the corn into ethanol, and the increased cost of corn that will affect the food market.

It is fundamental, however, to understand that the market is constantly adapting to the demands of consumers. As petroleum becomes more expensive, and as consumers become increasingly sensitive to the potential effects on the environment, alternative fuels will become economically viable. Ethanol appears to be a leading candidate to supplement petroleum use, though high tariffs on sugar-based ethanol (produced in Brazil and far more efficient than corn-based ethanol) may be an impediment. Manufacturers are also exploring hydrogen fuel cells with great fervor; and hybrid electrical cars have already made an appearance in the U.S. market.

Petroleum-based technologies have transformed the global economy.

The future of oil production and use depends on many factors, including demand, pressing environmental issues, and the availability of acceptable alternatives. Although considerable research is under way to develop the next generation of energy technologies, petroleum will likely maintain its position as a major source of energy in the short term.

Oil Is Vital to the World Economy

Terry Hathaway

Terry Hathaway is a contributing writer to Suite101.com, an independent, online information source.

Since the horse and carriage gave way to the car as the main method of transportation, oil has been vitally important to the world economy. Its importance has risen to the extent that in a world suddenly without oil, all the minor and major distribution systems that allow economic transactions on a more than local basis would fail and the world economy would collapse.

The Current Level of World Oil Consumption

According to the EIA [U.S. Energy Information Administration] the world currently consumes 85.64 million barrels of crude oil daily—roughly equivalent to every single person on the planet using 2 litres of oil a day. With the current market prices of a barrel of oil being $51, global consumption of oil costs $4.3 billion every single day, or 62 cents for every person.

Of course, the global distribution of oil consumption is not evenly spread out as developed and oil-rich states consume far more oil than less developed states. Also, all of this oil is not simply consumed with no end product. Oil is involved in the manufacture of a large number of everyday items, such as plastics, asphalt, or fertilizers.

However, the majority of this oil is refined into gasoline, jet fuel, and diesel, to be used for transportation. According to

Terry Hathaway, "Oil's Importance to the World Economy: A Look at the Current, and Future, Global Consumption of Gasoline," Suite101.com, March 30, 2009. www.suite101.com. © Terry Hathaway. Reproduced by permission of the author.

Ran Goel in his 2004 *New Political Economy* article, "A Bargain Born of Paradox", oil's role in fuelling transport oil is currently non-substitutable—there is nothing in the world that, within the bounds of its infrastructure, could replace oil.

Future World Oil Consumption

The world has experienced growth in its consumption of oil for the majority of the years since the early 1900s. This trend is likely to continue into the future with the majority of the growth in oil consumption coming from two sources—India and China.

In a world suddenly without oil, all the minor and major distribution systems that allow economic transactions . . . would fail and the world economy would collapse.

Together, these two countries account for over a third of the world's population—2.5 billion people—and have been following plans to allow each of them to rapidly economically develop.

The Rise in China's Oil Consumption

China's oil consumption has already risen from 2 million barrels per day (bpd) in 1990 to 6.93 million bpd now. Following this, the EIA estimates that Chinese oil consumption will rise to 15 million bpd by 2030—adding a further 8 million barrels, or around 10%, to the current world consumption.

However, if we consider that Chinese oil consumption currently stands at [less] than one litre [per person] a day, compared to the USA's 11 litres [per person per day], then we can begin to understand the potentially huge rise in oil consumption that China represents. In fact, if Chinese per capita consumption of oil rose to the same level as the USA, then the world's total oil consumption would double to over 160 million bpd.

India's Future Potential Oil Demands

India's oil consumption, reflecting its slower rate of economic growth, currently stands at 2.7 million bpd and is expected to grow to 4.5 million bpd by 2030. However, with India's huge, and growing, population, estimates of India's future oil consumption could easily be revised upwards based on small increases in predicted levels of economic growth.

Also, with the recent release of the 100,000-rupee ($2,000) Tata Nano car, with its aim of expanding the Indian car market by 65%, India's potential to drive up future world consumption of oil should not be underestimated.

The Oil and Natural Gas Industry Is an Essential Part of the U.S. Economy

Myra Crownover

Myra Crownover is a representative of District 64 in the Texas House of Representatives. She serves as the vice-chair of the Texas House Committee on Energy Resources.

The invisible hand of the marketplace is alive and well in Texas. Over the past 12 months Texas has created 245,000 jobs. That accounts for more than half of the jobs created in America during that time.

Not coincidentally, Texas has the second lowest tax burden of the 50 states. Even conservative estimates have projected a $10 billion surplus for the next biennium. Texas also leads the nation in energy production—30% of the natural gas and 20% of oil produced in America come from Texas.

So what can the rest of the nation learn from Texas when it comes to energy, the economy, and the environment?

The Example of Texas

There is debate in Congress right now as to whether the Atlantic and Pacific coastlines should be opened to offshore drilling. In Texas and the Gulf of Mexico, we have been producing millions of barrels of oil for years with no environmental consequences. Offshore drilling safety is so advanced that even during Hurricane Katrina not one drilling rig in the Gulf experienced a significant environmental event.

In 1989, Texas Parks and Wildlife collaborated with the oil and gas industry and the federal government to create the "Rigs to Reefs" program. Under the program, an oil company converts a decommissioned oil rig into an underwater reef. The companies pay the entire cost of the conversion and even donate a portion of the money they save back to Texas.

In Texas and the Gulf of Mexico, we have been producing millions of barrels of oil for years with no environmental consequences.

Since the program's inception, and at no cost to the state, Texas has added more than 100 healthy, vibrant, and productive reefs to our coastline where before there was an underwater mud plain. Texas has chosen to work with the industry instead of against it, and as a result, the Texas coast is cleaner and more productive than ever.

Another area where Texas leads the nation is in enhanced oil recovery [EOR]. In 1972, long before CO_2 was considered pollution, oil producers in Texas were treating it as a commodity. EOR works by pumping CO_2 into a depleted oil field to push out previously unrecoverable oil. The Texas government did not create this market. Instead, it got out of the way and allowed oil producers to find the most efficient way to extract additional oil. EOR now accounts for 20% of daily production in Texas.

Using conservative estimates, the benefits of EOR production will result in $200 billion in additional revenue and 1.5 million jobs created in Texas. The rest of the nation is catching on. The Department of Energy estimates that by using EOR technology, America could add 89 billion barrels of oil to its reserves leading to untold billions in potential economic growth—not to mention getting the United States closer to "energy independence."

The Texas marketplace also is on the cutting edge of other clean sources of energy. The EOR infrastructure already in place is attracting investment in another clean energy technology—carbon capture and storage [CCS]. A conventional fossil fuel power plant using CCS technology captures the CO_2 before it leaves the plant, instead of releasing it into the atmosphere. The CO_2 is then stored underground where it is sequestered for a millennia. This is an expensive addition to the cost of energy production. However, innovative entrepreneurs are planning to sell the CO_2 to EOR producers in order to lower the cost of production for both industries.

The Department of Energy estimates that by using EOR [enhanced oil recovery] technology, America could add 89 billion barrels of oil to its reserves.

Let the Market Work

The Texas government also stayed out of the market when times were bad. In the 1980s, when oil was $10 a barrel, we didn't bail out our producers. Many businesses failed and many fortunes were lost. However, the ones that survived were leaner, meaner, and more efficient. Unfortunately, in Washington, D.C., Congress is talking about a "windfall profits tax," which would punish the very producers we depend on. In Texas, we prefer to let the market work. Profit is the motivation that keeps oil flowing.

The concern over global warming is having a profound impact on how America will produce the energy it needs in the next century. Texas already produces more wind energy than any other state. By 2007, Texas installed wind capacity of 4,296 megawatts, enough to power about 1 million homes. On July 17, the Public Utility Commission of Texas approved a plan to add 18,456 megawatts of additional transmission capacity for wind power from rural West Texas to the metropolitan areas of the state.

When it comes to energy and the economy, we look at the industry as part of the solution, not part of the problem. So far, the results have been good.

America's Dependence on Middle Eastern Oil Was the Reason for the Iraq War

James Cogan

James Cogan is a staff writer for the World Socialist Web site, an Internet site that opposes the capitalist market system and promotes world socialism.

It is fitting that today's deadline [June 30, 2009] for the withdrawal of US troops from Iraq's cities coincides with a meeting in Baghdad to auction off some of the country's largest oil fields to companies such as ExxonMobil, Chevron and British Petroleum [BP]. It is a reminder of the real motives for the 2003 invasion and in whose interests over one million Iraqis and 4,634 American and other Western troops have been killed. The Iraq war was, and continues to be, an imperialist war waged by the American ruling elite for control of oil and geostrategic advantage.

The Iraq war was, and continues to be, an imperialist war waged by the American ruling elite for control of oil and geostrategic advantage.

The contracts will facilitate the first large-scale exploitation of Iraq's energy resources by US and other transnationals since the country's oil industry was nationalised in 1972. On offer are 20-year rights over six fields that hold more than five billion barrels of easily and cheaply extractable oil. In the autonomous Kurdish region of northern Iraq, where foreign companies are already operating, the Norwegian firm DNO is now producing so-called "sweet oil" from a relatively small field at Tawke, at a cost of less than $2 a barrel.

In an apt analogy, Larry Goldstein of the US-based Energy Policy Research Foundation told the *New York Times* last week: "Asking why oil companies are interested in Iraq is like asking why robbers rob banks—because that's where the money is." Iraq's total oil reserves are estimated to be at least 115 billion barrels. Its reserves of natural gas are at least 3.36 billion cubic metres.

The War's Carnage

Millions of people around the world understood in 2003 that the claims of the [George W.] Bush administration and its international allies about Iraqi weapons of mass destruction and links to terrorism were threadbare lies promulgated to justify the plunder of the country's oil wealth. The claim by the [Barack] Obama White House that it is continuing the occupation to consolidate "Iraqi democracy" is also a lie.

The war was driven by the decline of US global power and growing class tensions within the United States itself. The American capitalist elite believed that military domination in the Persian Gulf would give them access to lucrative resources, as well as a powerful lever against their main European and Asian rivals, who depend upon the region for critical supplies of energy. The militarist agitation surrounding the war was used to smother public disquiet and divert discontent away from the economic inequality that wracks American society.

The American capitalist elite believed that military domination in the Persian Gulf would give them access to lucrative [oil] resources.

It has taken more than six years of carnage—far longer than any pro-war analyst would have predicted—to establish the conditions where major corporations feel sufficiently confident to begin making substantial investments in Iraq's oil industry. Iraqi resistance to the US invasion had first to be drowned in blood and the population reduced to a state of terror and insecurity.

The war has produced a litany of crimes, from the torture policy at Abu Ghraib and other prisons, to the destruction of cities such as Fallujah and the attack on densely populated suburbs like Sadr City, to the unleashing of Shiite death squads to depopulate the centres of Sunni resistance in Baghdad.

The country has been economically ruined. Unemployment and underemployment stand at between 30 and 50 percent. At least seven million people live on less than $2 a day, and malnutrition and disease are rampant.

The Shiite fundamentalist–dominated Iraqi government of Prime Minister Nouri al-Maliki presides over the misery of the population in exchange for US backing. It now has a bloated US-equipped military and police apparatus of over 630,000 armed men.

Concerns About a US Withdrawal

The repression of the Iraqi masses was the basis for the withdrawal timetable that was agreed to by the Bush administration in last year's Status of Forces Agreement (SOFA). US forces are deemed no longer needed to perform the frontline operations against what remains of the anti-occupation insurgency. Instead, units of the Iraqi army are to take over those tasks.

The bulk of the 130,000 American troops in Iraq have been pulled back to heavily fortified camps on the outskirts of the cities, or to the massive air bases that have been built at places such as Balad and Tallil. The SOFA permits them to remain until December 2011, by which time new arrangements for the long-term presence of US forces will have been worked out.

American commanders, while outwardly optimistic, have not been able to hide their apprehension over the withdrawal from the cities. To shore up the Iraqi army, some 10,000 US troops are currently embedded as "trainers" in its ranks—a number that will increase to over 50,000 over the coming months. Baghdad's western suburbs have been creatively categorised as "outside" the urban area. Aircraft, helicopter gunships, artillery and rapid response units are on constant standby to assist Iraqi forces when needed.

It has taken more than six years of carnage . . . to establish the conditions where major corporations feel sufficiently confident to begin making substantial investments in Iraq's oil industry.

The concerns are not only that insurgent groups will take advantage of the US withdrawal to regroup in Iraq's cities and resume significant resistance to both the al-Maliki government and American troops. Both Washington and its puppet government are worried that the social plight of the Iraqi working class and popular opposition to the concessions al-Maliki is making to US imperialism and foreign capital could give rise to large-scale protests and unrest.

The Obama administration is acutely conscious that a large majority of Iraqis bitterly opposes the US presence in the country. Behind the scenes, it is reportedly pressuring al-Maliki to abandon a promise to hold a referendum on the Status of Forces Agreement, knowing that it would be overwhelmingly rejected.

There are also sharp disputes between the rival Shiite, Sunni and Kurdish factions of the Iraqi ruling elite over the allocation of oil revenues and other sources of wealth. The most explosive tensions centre on the insistence of the Kurdish autonomous region that it get control of the northern oil fields around the city of Kirkuk—two of which are among the six fields being offered for contract in this week's auction.

The Kurdish [Kurdistan] Regional Government (KRG) last week denounced the auction as "unconstitutional" and warned that companies are "ill-advised" to enter into any contract in Kirkuk to which the KRG is not also a party. The outbreak of an ethnic civil war in the north cannot be ruled out, nor can US military operations to suppress such a development.

US imperialism faces a debacle of its own making in Iraq. Amidst the meltdown of economic activity internationally, and the escalation of the US war in Afghanistan and its proxy war in Pakistan, a large proportion of the American military is still tied down by the conflict in Iraq and there is no end in sight. The Obama administration is nevertheless committed to continuing the occupation and realising the predatory objectives of the invasion—in which oil has always loomed large.

Oil Wealth Fuels Conflict Within Oil-Producing Countries

Michael L. Ross

Michael L. Ross is a political science professor at the University of California, Los Angeles, and the director of the Center for Southeast Asian Studies.

The world is far more peaceful today than it was 15 years ago. There were 17 major civil wars—with "major" meaning the kind that kill more than a thousand people a year—going on at the end of the Cold War; by 2006, there were just five. During that period, the number of smaller conflicts also fell, from 33 to 27.

Despite this trend, there has been no drop in the number of wars in countries that produce oil. The main reason is that oil wealth often wreaks havoc on a country's economy and politics, makes it easier for insurgents to fund their rebellions, and aggravates ethnic grievances. Today, with violence falling in general, oil-producing states make up a growing fraction of the world's conflict-ridden countries. They now host about a third of the world's civil wars, both large and small, up from one-fifth in 1992. According to some, the U.S.-led invasion of Iraq shows that oil breeds conflict between countries, but the more widespread problem is that it breeds conflict within them.

The number of oil-producer-based conflicts is likely to grow in the future as stratospheric prices of crude oil push more countries in the developing world to produce oil and gas. In 2001, the [George W.] Bush administration's energy

Michael L. Ross, "Blood Barrels: Why Oil Wealth Fuels Conflict," *Foreign Affairs*, vol. 87, no. 3, May–June 2008, p. 2–8. Copyright © 2008 by the Council on Foreign Relations, Inc. Reproduced by permission of the publisher, www.foreignaffairs.com.

task force hailed the emergence of new producers as a chance for the United States to diversify the sources of its energy imports and reduce its reliance on oil from the Persian Gulf. More than a dozen countries in Africa, the Caspian basin, and Southeast Asia have recently become, or will soon become, significant oil and gas exporters. Some of these countries, including Chad, East Timor, and Myanmar, have already suffered internal strife. Most of the rest are poor, undemocratic, and badly governed, which means that they are likely to experience violence as well. On top of that, record oil prices will yield the kind of economic windfalls that typically produce further unrest.

The number of oil-producer-based conflicts is likely to grow in the future as stratospheric prices of crude oil push more countries in the developing world to produce oil and gas.

Oil is not unique; diamonds and other minerals produce similar problems. But as the world's most sought-after commodity, and with more countries dependent on it than on gold, copper, or any other resource, oil has an impact more pronounced and more widespread.

The Curse

The oil booms of the 1970s brought great wealth—and later great anguish—to many petroleum-rich countries in the developing world. In the 1970s, oil-producing states enjoyed fast economic growth. But in the following three decades, many suffered crushing debt, high unemployment, and sluggish or declining economies. At least half of the members of OPEC (the Organization of [the] Petroleum Exporting Countries) were poorer in 2005 than they had been 30 years earlier. Oil-rich countries that once held great promise, such as Algeria and Nigeria, have unraveled as a result of decades of internal conflict.

At least half of the members of OPEC (the Organization of [the] Petroleum Exporting Countries) were poorer in 2005 than they had been 30 years earlier.

These states were plagued by the so-called oil curse. One aspect of the problem is an economic syndrome known as Dutch disease, named after the troubles that beset the Netherlands in the 1960s after it discovered natural gas in the North Sea. The affliction hits when a country becomes a significant producer and exporter of natural resources. Rising resource exports push up the value of the country's currency, which makes its other exports, such as manufactured and agricultural goods, less competitive abroad. Export figures for those products then decline, depriving the country of the benefits of dynamic manufacturing and agricultural bases and leaving it dependent on its resource sector and so at the mercy of often volatile international markets. In Nigeria, for example, the oil boom of the early 1970s caused agricultural exports to drop from 11.2 percent of GDP [gross domestic product, the measure of a country's total economic output] in 1968 to 2.8 percent of GDP in 1972; the country has yet to recover.

Another facet of the oil curse is the sudden glut of revenues. Few oil-rich countries have the fiscal discipline to invest the windfalls prudently; most squander them on wasteful projects. The governments of Kazakhstan and Nigeria, for example, have spent their petroleum incomes on building new capital cities while failing to bring running water to the many villages throughout their countries that lack it. Well-governed states with highly educated populations and diverse economies, such as Canada and Norway, have avoided these ill ef-

in any country, but because oil prices are unusually
[vo]le, oil-producing countries tend to be battered by cycles
[b]ooms and busts. And the more dependent a government
[is on] its oil revenues, the more likely it is to face turmoil
[when] prices go south.

[Se]cond, oil wealth often helps support insurgencies. Rebel-
[lions] in many countries fail when their instigators run out of
[cash]. But raising money in petroleum-rich countries is rela-
[tively] easy: Insurgents can steal oil and sell it on the black
[mark]et (as has happened in Iraq and Nigeria), extort money
[from] oil companies working in remote areas (as in Colombia
[and S]udan), or find business partners to fund them in ex-
[chan]ge for future consideration in the event they seize power
[(as in] Equatorial Guinea and the Republic of the Congo).

---

*[O]il revenues tend to increase corruption, strengthen the
[ha]nds of dictators, and weaken new democracies.*

[T]hird, oil wealth encourages separatism. Oil and gas are
[usual]ly produced in self-contained economic enclaves that
[yield] a lot of revenue for the central government but provide
[few j]obs for locals—who also often bear the costs of petro-
[leum] development, such as lost property rights and environ-
[menta]l damage. To reverse the imbalance, some locals seek
[auton]omy from the central government, as have the people in
[the pe]troleum-rich regions of Bolivia, Indonesia, Iran, Iraq,
[Niger]ia, and Sudan.

[Th]is is not to say that petroleum is the only source of
[these] conflicts or that it inevitably breeds violence. In fact, al-
[most] half of all the states that have produced oil since 1970
[have b]een conflict-free. Oil alone cannot create conflict, but it
[often] exacerbates latent tensions and gives governments and
[their] more militant opponents the means to fight them out.
[Gover]nments that limit corruption and put their windfalls to
[good] use rarely face unrest. Unfortunately, oil production is

fects. But many more oil-rich countries hav
less effective governments and so are more
oil curse.

Few oil-rich countries have the fiscal dis
the windfalls prudently; most squander t
projects.

Oil wealth also has political downsides
ten worse than the economic ones. Oil re
crease corruption, strengthen the hands
weaken new democracies. The more mon
of Iran, Russia, and Venezuela have receiv
exports, the less accountable they have b
citizens—and the easier it has been for
buy off their opponents. A major boom i
the one that took the price of a barrel fr
February 1999 to over $100 in March 200
danger.

Oil on Fire

For new oil and gas producers, the graves
bility of armed conflict. Among developi
producing country is twice as likely to su
as a non-oil-producing one. The conflicts
from low-level secessionist struggles, suc
in the Niger Delta and southern Thailan
wars, such as in Algeria, Colombia, Su
Iraq.

Oil wealth can trigger conflict in thr
cause economic instability, which then le
bility. When people lose their jobs, ... [
frustrated with their government and m
ing recruited by rebel armies that chall
government. A sudden drop in income

now rising precisely in those countries where wise leadership is often in short supply. Most of the new energy-rich states are in Africa (Chad, Côte d'Ivoire, Mauritania, Namibia, and São Tomé and Príncipe), the Caspian basin (Azerbaijan, Kazakhstan, and Turkmenistan), or Southeast Asia (Cambodia, East Timor, Myanmar, and Vietnam). Almost all are undemocratic. The majority are very poor and ill-equipped to manage a sudden and large influx of revenues. And many also have limited petroleum reserves—just enough to yield large revenues for a decade or two—which means that if they succumb to civil war, they will squander whatever chance they had of using their oil windfalls to escape from poverty.

For new oil and gas producers, the gravest danger is the possibility of armed conflict.

Curtailing Violence

Since the early 1990s, the international community has developed an effective set of tools for ending insurrections. These include cutting off foreign aid to rebel groups, using diplomatic and economic sanctions to bring governments to the negotiating table, and deploying peacekeeping forces to monitor any agreements that might result from the pressure. Combined with the demise of the Soviet Union, such methods helped reduce the number of civil wars in non-oil-producing countries by over 85 percent between 1992 and 2006. . . .

Curtailing rebellions in oil-producing states will be harder. The world's thirst for oil immunizes petroleum-rich governments from the kind of pressures that might otherwise force them to the bargaining table. Since these governments' coffers are already overflowing, aid means little to them. They can readily buy friends in powerful places and therefore have little fear of sanctions from the UN [United Nations] Security Council. In any event, the growing appetite of oil-importing countries for new supplies makes it easy for exporters to bypass such restrictions. The government of President Omar al-Bashir has used Sudan's oil sales to China to deflect diplomatic pressure from Western states asking it to stop the killings in Darfur. Myanmar's military government is following the same strategy: In exchange for Myanmar's selling its natural gas to China, Beijing is blocking tougher sanctions against the junta [government ruled by the military] in the UN Security Council.

The best solution would be for rich countries to sharply reduce their consumption of oil and gas and help poor countries find a more sustainable path out of poverty than oil production. But the Western economies are so dependent on fossil fuels and the demand for oil and gas imports in China and India is growing so quickly that even the most aggressive push for alternatives would take decades to have any effect. In the meantime, a different approach is needed.

Undoing the "Oil Curse"

No single initiative will undo the oil curse and bring peace to oil-producing states, but four measures can help. The first would be to cut off funding to insurgents who profit from the oil trade. Oil-importing states could contribute by refusing to buy oil that comes from concessions sold by insurgents. Both the insurrection in the Republic of the Congo in 1997 and the 2004 coup attempt in Equatorial Guinea were financed by investors hoping to win oil contracts from the rebels once they controlled the government. A ban on oil stemming from these transactions, much like the ban on conflict diamonds, could help prevent such rebellions in the future.

A second way to limit the effects of the oil curse would be to encourage the governments of resource-rich states to be more transparent. Their national budgets are unusually opaque; this facilitates corruption and reduces public confidence in the state, two conditions that tend to breed conflict. The Extractive Industries Transparency Initiative [EITI], an effort launched by nongovernmental organizations in 2002 and expanded by former British Prime Minister Tony Blair, encourages oil and mining companies to "publish what they pay" and governments to "disclose what they receive." This is a good idea, but it is not enough. Adherence to the EITI's reporting standards is voluntary, and although 24 countries have pledged to adopt them, none has fully complied yet. It is important that they do and that the effort to promote transparency be expanded. Oil-importing states, such as the United States, should insist, for example, that energy companies also "publish what they pump"—that is, disclose from which countries their petroleum originates. This would give consumers the power to reward the most responsible companies. And that, in turn, would give companies an incentive to improve the conditions in oil-producing regions.

Another problem with the current standards is that even though exporting governments are pressured to disclose the revenues they collect, they are not expected to reveal how they spend the money. Oil revenues often vanish into the nooks of state-owned oil companies or into governments' off-budget accounts. According to the International Monetary Fund, between 1997 and 2002, the Angolan government accrued at least $4.2 billion in oil receipts that it could not account for; at the time, Angola had the fifth-highest infant mortality rate in the world.

One possible remedy would be for the EITI (or a similar effort) to develop guidelines for the transparent allocation of all revenues from extractive industries. In his recent book *The Bottom Billion*, the economist Paul Collier suggests creating a "natural resources charter" that would set international standards for the governance of natural-resource revenues. The charter would help citizens figure out if their governments are properly managing the wealth. International credit-rating agencies could also use it to assess governments' creditworthiness, which would give governments a financial incentive to abide by the charter.

A third way to help oil-exporting states cast off the oil curse would be to help them better manage the flow of their oil revenues. Since the earliest days of the oil business in the mid-nineteenth century, oil prices have alternately soared and crashed. There is no reason to think this will change. But nor is there any reason to assume that because oil prices are volatile a government's oil revenues must be too. In a typical oil contract, the oil company is guaranteed a steady income and the government gets to keep most of the profits but also must bear most of the risk of fluctuating prices. This setup is exactly backward. International oil companies are skilled at smoothing out their income flows—putting money aside in fat years to spend in lean ones—whereas governments are terrible at it. The terms of these contracts should be changed so that the oil companies bear more of the price risk than they do now and governments bear less.

Helping oil-rich countries avoid violent conflicts and, more broadly, escape the oil curse will not be easy.

Even with greater transparency and steadier revenues, many low-income countries simply lack the capacity to translate oil wealth into roads, schools, and health clinics. For these, the best way to steer clear of the oil curse may not be to sell oil for cash at all, but to trade it directly for the goods and services their people need. The governments of Angola and Nigeria are now experimenting with this type of barter: They have awarded oil contracts to Chinese companies in exchange for the construction of infrastructure. Western oil companies have been reluctant to make similar deals, pointing out that they know little about building railroads and have trouble competing against state-owned enterprises in this arena, such as the Chinese oil companies. But they could easily team up with reputable companies that could carry out the work. And why stop at infrastructure? By forming partnerships with experienced service providers, oil companies could pay back host countries by, say, conducting antimalarial campaigns or building schools, irrigation projects, or microfinancing facilities. As more companies bid for such "oil-for-development" contracts, the terms of the contracts would become better for the governments. If inexperienced governments need help carrying out these auctions, the World Bank, or other international organizations, could provide technical assistance....

Helping oil-rich countries avoid violent conflicts and, more broadly, escape the oil curse will not be easy. Many of their governments are indifferent to the incentives offered by diplomats and development specialists. On the other hand, if the main stakeholders—oil producers and energy companies, as well as international organizations, oil importers, and consumers—do not find better remedies, a whole new set of countries will suffer the same tragic fate as Angola, Nigeria, Sudan, and, yes, even Iraq.

Oil Wealth Sustains Oil Tyrannies Around the World

Alvaro Vargas Llosa

Alvaro Vargas Llosa is a senior fellow of the Center on Global Prosperity at the Independent Institute, a nonprofit research and educational organization. He is also an author and a nationally syndicated columnist for the Washington Post Writers Group, a syndication service run by the Washington Post *newspaper.*

Recessions can be a good thing—they wring the excesses out of the economy and focus people's attention on public policy mistakes that often are the root causes of investment bubbles. Many people thought that this particular recession would offer another kind of benefit. By bringing oil prices back to earth, it was supposed to debilitate the autocracies, from Russia to Iran to Venezuela, that depend on them.

This has not happened. Oil prices dropped 80 percent in the early stages of the recession, but had climbed back to $70 a barrel by June. Their sails have since lost a bit of wind, but the prospects, even if the recession lasts long, point to sustained high prices.

Conspiracy theories abound when it comes to crude, but the simple truth is that oil prices are driven by the market. As has been evident for some time, the supply coming out of existing production is diminishing, and the (very few) new discoveries are not expected to make up for the imbalance, especially given the insatiable demand from emerging economies.

This is bad news for those who were hoping that the likes of Vladimir Putin, Mahmoud Ahmadinejad and Hugo Chávez would see their coffers depleted anytime soon. And herein lies a cruel paradox. Part of the reason supply has not been able to keep up with skyrocketing demand is the sheer inefficiency and the rampant corruption of state-controlled oil companies; the list includes Russia (where production fell in 2008), Iran (where gasoline has been rationed since 2007) and Venezuela (where daily output has dropped by 1 million barrels), and also countries such as Mexico, where the political system is democratic but where oil is a government monopoly. The regimes that have caused shortages in the world supply of the commodity on which their dictatorships depend are now reaping the benefits of higher prices partly caused by their own incompetence.

The proposition that a sustained drop in oil revenues will topple an autocratic government is highly debatable.

Occasionally, as happened when the massive Tupi oil fields were found in Brazil's Santos Basin at the end of 2007, there is speculation that production imbalances will be corrected. But—apart from the obvious fact that exploitation takes many years—the markets do not really expect Tupi and other potential discoveries to offset the decline of existing production in oil-rich tyrannies—or the dwindling reserves in more palatable political environments such as North Sea oil countries.

The proposition that a sustained drop in oil revenues will topple an autocratic government is highly debatable. Indeed there are many examples of dictatorships that have survived and even strengthened themselves in the face of adverse economic fortunes. North Korea's Kim Il-Sung turned his country's economy, which was far more developed than that of South Korea at the end of the Korean War, into a medieval autarchy of sorts while he consolidated his totalitarian power. Cuba's Fidel Castro was not weakened one bit after the collapse of the Soviet Union brought an end to Moscow's subsidies and Havana launched what it called the Special Period, essentially a descent into a pre-industrial subsistence economy.

But if there is no certainty that an autocracy will be threatened by the demise of its sources of revenue, it is clearly the case that the sustainability of those sources will make things much easier for the autocrat. The reason is simple. The availability of abundant cash enables the dictator to bribe the regime's elite, to lull a significant portion of the population into submission, and, when the hunger for power extends beyond the country's borders, to sustain client states. The absence of cash greatly increases the need to maintain an efficient police state whose primary purpose is to spy on those who are close to power and instill paralyzing fear throughout society. All dictatorships do some of this, but they can make up for their own repressive inefficiency with cash used to buy loyalties and fund redistributive populism.

The availability of abundant cash enables the dictator to bribe the regime's elite, to lull a significant portion of the population into submission, and . . . to sustain client states.

The realities of the market, and probably the expectation of inflation caused by the printing of money in the United States and the rest of the world during the current recession, virtually guarantee that oil tyrannies in the Middle East, Eurasia and Latin America will continue to enjoy big revenues. Those seeking to topple them will need to take into account this sobering fact when putting together their strategies.

CHAPTER 2

How Has the World's Reliance on Oil Affected the Environment?

Chapter Preface

One of the worst environmental disasters in U.S. history was the *Exxon Valdez* oil spill off the coast of Alaska in 1989. The spill occurred just after midnight on March 24, 1989, when the oil tanker *Exxon Valdez* slammed into a reef. This accident released 10.8 million gallons of crude oil into the secluded and once pristine Prince William Sound and created an oil slick that eventually covered eleven thousand miles of ocean waters. Oil also spread along thirteen hundred miles of shoreline, in the process polluting a national forest, two national parks, two national wildlife refuges, five state parks, four important state habitat areas, one state game sanctuary, and many ancestral lands of Alaskan natives. The toxic oil immediately killed 250,000 sea birds, 2,800 sea otters, 300 harbor seals, 250 bald eagles, up to 22 orcas, and billions of salmon and herring eggs. The disaster also damaged the local economy and destroyed the livelihoods of fishermen and other residents.

At the time of the accident, the *Exxon Valdez* was traveling from the Valdez oil terminal in Alaska to Long Beach, California. The ship's captain, Joseph Hazelwood, explained later that he had moved the ship out of the shipping lane to avoid ice. Sometime after 11 P.M., Hazelwood placed crew members Gregory Cousins and Robert Kagan in charge of steering the ship, even though neither had been given the mandatory six hours off duty before their twelve-hour shift began. The ship was on autopilot, but Hazelwood left instructions on when it should be returned to the shipping lane—a violation of company rules. Hazelwood, an alcoholic, also admitted to drinking alcohol prior to the accident.

A massive cleanup operation was launched by Exxon Mobil, the company that owned the tanker, but twenty years later the affected areas still have not been completely cleaned up.

Studies have shown that oil remains at many sites, and oil exposure is still affecting many shore-dwelling species. For example, killer whale numbers continue to decline; sea otters and seabird populations have not recovered to pre-spill numbers; and the herring fish population, a species vital to the marine food chain that once supported a vibrant commercial fishery, is still experiencing significant problems. According to the *Exxon Valdez* Oil Spill Trustee Council, the group charged with monitoring damage to the environment, the remaining oil will take decades and possibly centuries to disappear completely. In addition, many commentators have criticized Exxon's slow response and the methods it used for cleanup. The company initially tried to disperse the oil rather than corral it, and when it did begin cleaning the oil from beaches and rocks, it used high-pressure hot water. This action, critics said, destroyed microbial populations that were essential to the marine food chain and that could have helped to biodegrade the oil. In some ways, therefore, the cleanup made things worse.

Exxon Mobil was fined millions of dollars as a result of the oil spill. In a 1991 plea agreement with the government, the company agreed to pay the largest criminal pollution fine ever imposed—$150 million (although $125 million of this was later forgiven in recognition of the company's cooperation in cleanup efforts). Exxon also agreed to pay $100 million for damage to wildlife and an additional $100 million for unanticipated damages unknown at the time of the settlement. Finally, the company agreed to pay $900 million in ten annual installments to Alaska and the federal government for restoration of the site. In 1994 a jury awarded victims of the oil spill $5 billion in punitive damages in a case brought by a group of thirty-three thousand commercial fishermen, cannery workers, native Alaskans, and others affected by the disaster. Exxon, however, appealed the punitive damages award all the way to the U.S. Supreme Court, where the company won a favorable decision that cut the punitive damages to $507.5 million in

June 2008. The Court found that the damage award was excessive and that it should not exceed the amount already paid by the company in compensatory damages. The ruling gives each surviving plaintiff about $15,000 each, compared to $75,000, which they each would have received if the Court had upheld the damage award.

In response to the spill, the U.S. Congress passed the Oil Pollution Act of 1990, a law that prohibits any ships that have caused an oil spill of more than one million U.S. gallons (3,800 m³) in any marine area from operating in Prince William Sound. The Oil Pollution Act also called for the gradual phase-in of double hull designs for oil tankers. Such a design would prevent many oil spills, and in the case of the *Exxon Valdez*, would likely have significantly reduced the amount of oil spilled. Exxon sought to overturn the law, arguing that it was a bill of attainder (that is, a law designed to punish a specific party without a trial), but the federal court ruled against Exxon.

March 24, 2009, marked the twentieth anniversary of the *Exxon Valdez* disaster, but state and federal governments have yet to collect millions of dollars that Exxon promised to pay. On June 1, 2006, the federal government notified Exxon Mobil that, based on the continued presence of oil in the Prince William Sound region, it would need to pay an additional $92 million to fund continuing restoration projects. The company failed to respond to the government's demand, however, and the claim remains unsatisfied. Neither the administration of former president George W. Bush nor Alaska's former governor Sarah Palin made any effort to collect these monies, and it remains to be seen whether President Barack Obama will pursue the matter.

The viewpoints in this chapter address the environmental damage caused by oil spills and other aspects of the oil drilling, production, and transportation process.

A Century of Oil Has Taken a Heavy Toll on the Environment

Union of Concerned Scientists

The Union of Concerned Scientists is a science-based, nonprofit organization working for a healthy environment and a safer world.

Oil has been a defining force in the 20th century. Oil has shaped political boundaries, defined the outcome of battles and wars, created and disrupted economies, and remade the urban environment. It has also taken a heavy toll on the environment, through air pollution and oil spills.

We are burning through our supplies of oil so quickly that oil may become a uniquely 20th-century phenomenon. American oil production is fading fast, even as demand rises. Worldwide reserves of oil could supply 40 to 60 years of consumption at current rates. By the middle of the 21st century, world oil supplies could be dwindling. Environmental pressures may lead to restrictions on its use before then.

How Oil Is Formed

Oil is formed from ancient plants and animals deposited since the Cambrian period 500 million years ago. This organic matter settled on the sea floors of that era, mixing with and being covered by sedimentary rocks, mostly sandstone and limestone. Over many years, deposits of more sediments, tectonic plate movements or volcanic activity buried these deposits under an impermeable layer of stone or mud.

Trapped under high pressure, with no oxygen present, bacteria broke down the dead plants and animals into hydrocarbons, such as coal, oil and natural gas. Once formed in this sedimentary layer, oil can be squeezed out or washed out by underground water flows. Since natural gas is less dense than oil, and oil is less dense than water, the gas tends to float on top, with oil under it, supported by water.

Although oil drilling and extraction can lead to ... groundwater contamination, the worst impacts from oil use are at the shipping, refining and use stages of the process.

Oil is not actually in pools underground; it is held in permeable rock, such as sandstone or ancient coral reefs, like a sponge. Gas, oil and water would rise to the surface over time, but they are held underground by a "cap rock" such as a layer of shale. Oil and gas become concentrated in areas where there are high spots, or domes, under the layer of cap rock.

The most common type of oil trap occurs in an "anticline." Anticlines are formed when the cap rock is buckled by geological movement, as when mountains are formed. The most recent major anticline formation was 20 million years ago, when the Alps, the Himalayas and the Rocky Mountains were formed.

How Oil Is Found: 3-D Seismic Analysis

The first method of prospecting for oil was no more complicated than finding oil seeping out of the ground. In places where the cap rock is thin, such as in parts of Iran and Kuwait, oil and gas leak from their reservoirs onto the surface. It is suspected that the famous "burning bush" of the biblical era was in fact a natural gas leak that ignited.

In West Virginia in the first half of the 19th century, water drills would routinely bring up water contaminated with oil.

This "rock oil" was considered to have some medicinal values, but no practical application. But due to the decline of the whaling industry in the 1850s, and the beginning of the industrial revolution, a new source of fuel was needed to replace whale oil for lamps. Suddenly Appalachian rock oil was worth more than water.

In 1859, the first oil well was drilled near Titusville, Pennsylvania, striking oil at 69.5 feet. After looking for seepages, the first method of oil exploration was to look for geographical features on the surface that suggested a possible anticline below. Exploration teams scoured the countryside on foot and mule back, mapping promising areas. When a good location was found, a shallow well was sunk. If oil was found, a mad rush was sure to follow.

Until 1919, surface mapping and study of surface rocks, followed by a typically unsuccessful exploratory well, was the only way to find oil. That year, the first seismic prospecting was begun in Europe. Seismic prospecting involves setting off an explosive shock at the surface and monitoring the speed of the shock waves that bounce off the geological structures below. A series of listening devices, called "geophones," are set at fixed distances away from the shock; they record the strength and timing of the signal.

Given the limited data processing capabilities of the day, only major formations could be found with seismic prospecting. But with a number of computer-aided refinements, this method is still in use today. By using high-powered computers, exploration geologists can set out even more geophones, analyze more shock wave trajectory possibilities, and look deeper into the earth with greater accuracy. After the data are analyzed, the results are displayed in three-dimensional color. Yet despite all this technology, wells are not always successful. As the saying goes, the only way to discover oil is with a drill.

How Oil Is Drilled

The first oil well, in Titusville, was a "cable tool rig." A heavy iron bit, tipped with steel, was suspended by a cable from a drilling derrick and repeatedly smashed into the ground. After it broke through the rock for a while, it was hoisted out and a "bailer" was dropped down the hole to remove the rock fragments. Although laborious and slow, this method was still used as late as the 1960s for shallow wells in rocky areas.

Oil intentionally released from Kuwaiti refineries and terminals by Iraqi troops amounted to 250 million gallons.

Rotary drills are more common today. Although some rotary drills were in operation for water wells as early as 1823, the method did not become widespread in the U.S. until 1900. By 1930s it was the dominant form of drilling, used extensively in the deep wells of Oklahoma, Texas and California.

In a rotary drill, a sharp tip of diamonds embedded in hardened steel bites into the ground, connected to motors on the surface by a long string of drilling pipes. The pipes, about 30 feet long each, are screwed together into strings as long as 24,000 feet, weighing up to 100 tons. Muddy water is pumped down through the drilling pipes to carry the chips of rock cut by the drill back to the surface. A battery of internal combustion or electric motors powers the rig.

Environmental Impacts of Oil Shipping and Use

After oil is brought to the surface, it is piped away from the rig to waiting boats or refineries. Crude oil from the Middle East is shipped by tanker ships to Europe, the US and the Pacific Rim. At 400 meters long, with a cargo capacity of 500,000 tons, supertankers are the largest moving things ever built.

The 6,600 boats in operation carry 524 billion gallons of oil every year. Each year, about 200 tankers load up at the port of Valdez, the outlet for the Alaska pipeline. Houston and New York are the busiest US ports, each receiving four or five tankers a day of imported oil.

Although oil drilling and extraction can lead to environmental problems, like groundwater contamination, the worst impacts from oil use are at the shipping, refining and use stages of the process. The most graphic type of impact is an oil spill. Between 1973 and 1993, there were over 200,000 oil spills in US waters, dumping over 230 million gallons of oil. Incredibly, that is an average of 28 "incidents" per day, spilling 31,000 gallons of oil every day for 20 years into our waterways.

The National Research Council estimates that almost a billion gallons of oil are spilled into the world's oceans and waterways each year.

Before supertankers, smaller ships were used to transport refined oil products, like gasoline and heating oil. Because these products are lighter than crude oil, they tend to evaporate when they are spilled. When crude oil is spilled in water, it quickly spreads out on top of the water. The *Exxon Valdez* spill covered 1,300 square miles of water and coastline. When birds land on the water, their feathers are coated with oil, causing them to sink and drown. Crude oil spilled in coastal areas can destroy coral reefs and mangrove swamps.

While the *Exxon Valdez* spill was the largest single spill in American waters and an unparalleled ecological disaster, it was only 11 million gallons. By comparison, oil intentionally released from Kuwaiti refineries and terminals by Iraqi troops amounted to 250 million gallons. In addition, they lit more than 700 oil wells, putting hundreds of tons of smoke and toxic chemicals into the air. In a list of the world's largest oil spills between 1967 and 1992, the *Exxon Valdez* spill ranks as number 36.

The National Research Council estimates that almost a billion gallons of oil are spilled into the world's oceans and waterways each year. And as bad as tanker spills can be, they amount to only 13 percent of the total oil lost. Municipal and industrial wastes, urban runoff, leaking pipelines and storage tanks and standard tanker operations, such as dumping ballast water, all contribute to marine pollution.

And as bad as marine pollution can be, air pollution from oil is even worse. Transportation accounts for half of nitrogen oxide emissions in the US, and a third of carbon dioxide emissions, and a host of other air emissions, including carbon monoxide, ozone, sulfur oxides, particulates, volatile organic compounds, methane and toxic metals. These emissions contribute to urban smog, acid rain and global warming, causing health problems in humans and animals, damage to crops, forests and buildings, degradation of habitat . . . the list seems endless.

One of the worst culprits in causing air and water pollution from oil is not some large corporation—it is each and every one of us who owns and drives a car.

Unfortunately, one of the worst culprits in causing air and water pollution from oil is not some large corporation—it is each and every one of us who owns and drives a car. Gas evaporates as we pump it into our cars, and when we spill it on the ground, contributing to smog. Oil drips from our engines, and finds its way into lakes and rivers. We drive increasingly large and inefficient cars an ever greater distance every year.

While carmakers and gas producers bear some responsibility in reducing our dependence on polluting oil, we must also take some personal responsibility. The solution to pollution is you.

Current Use of Oil

America now accounts for over 25 percent of the world's oil consumption, about 17 million barrels of oil per day. At the same time, we produce only 13 percent of the world's total. Two-thirds of the oil used in the US goes for transportation. The US gets about 40 percent of its primary energy from oil.

For every year since 1994, over half the oil we use has [been] imported. If we were to rely solely on American oil, our reserves would be depleted within 15 years. US oil production has been declining steadily since the early 1980s as fields are exhausted. New discoveries of oil in the US have also been declining, leading experts to believe that no new large sources of oil can be expected.

In inflation-adjusted dollars, gasoline prices are lower now than they have ever been in America, while the total state and federal gas tax is almost unchanged since the 1940s. In 1980, during the second oil crisis, a gallon of gasoline cost twice what it does today. Even in the auto-loving 1950s, when cars got less than half the mileage they get today, drivers paid more than 50 cents more per gallon than we do now.

It's little wonder, then, that oil consumption in the US is rapidly outpacing domestic oil production, and has steadily risen since the mid-1980s. If it weren't for the improved fuel economy of cars that resulted from the federal fuel efficiency standards (CAFE [Corporate Average Fuel Economy] standards), oil consumption would be much worse. In recent years, as large and inefficient sport-utility vehicles have been adopted as family cars, oil consumption is on the rise again.

The Future

Worldwide, oil accounts for about 40 percent of the primary energy produced. At current rates of production, about 65 million barrels per day, world oil supplies are predicted to last 60 to 70 years. Although discovery and extraction technologies may improve, pushing that date back, demand is likely to rise too, resulting in a quicker exhaustion.

Long before the world actually runs out of oil, there are likely to be major price fluctuations as supplies grow scarce. These fluctuations have proven to be extremely damaging to countries [that] are dependent on oil, like the US. When the OPEC [Organization of the Petroleum Exporting Countries] oil embargo happened in the 1970s, the US imported about 37 percent of the oil we use, two-thirds of this coming from OPEC countries, which controlled about 36 percent of the world market for oil. Now, although OPEC doesn't have the dominating control it once had, the US is even more dependent on imports, importing more than half our oil every year since 1994. About half of this oil comes from OPEC countries, primarily Saudi Arabia and Venezuela.

While economic disruptions and resource depletion are bound to happen sooner or later, the environmental burden of oil demands that we change our energy habits long before then. Above all, global warming requires a shift to cleaner and more efficient technologies.

While economic disruptions and resource depletion are bound to happen sooner or later, the environmental burden of oil demands that we change our energy habits long before then.

Two main approaches will encourage more responsible use of oil in the future—new transportation technologies and more accurate pricing of the costs of transportation.

New Technologies

In recent years there has been something of a design renaissance for cars and trucks, with electric, fuel cell and hybrid cars coming to showroom floors.

Battery, fuel cell, and hybrid vehicles use electrical motors, rather than a mechanical transmission, offering substantial efficiency improvements over the drivetrain of conventional vehicles.

Battery-powered vehicles use chemical batteries to store electricity for the vehicle, generated at power plants. Most power in the US comes from coal and nuclear fuels, though cleaner sources like wind, solar, geothermal and biomass offer a more sustainable path. Fuel cell and hybrid vehicles generate their electricity from liquid and gaseous fuels right on board. While these vehicles could use petroleum-derived products like gasoline and methanol, they could also use renewable fuels like ethanol, or even hydrogen.

Even using oil-based fuels, these advanced vehicles produce zero or near-zero tailpipe emissions. When the electricity and fuels used in electric vehicles are produced from renewable energy sources, advanced vehicles offer additional reductions in fossil fuel energy consumption and in emissions of carbon dioxide.

Proper Pricing

A more fundamental problem with oil is that the cost to consumers of owning and operating a car does not reflect its full price to society. Drivers do not directly pay the monetary costs of global warming, air pollution, water pollution, and oil dependence. Instead, everyone pays for the impacts on public health and the US economy.

Some pricing solutions include having drivers buy car insurance on a per-use basis by paying for it at the fuel pump, raising tolls on congested bridges and roads during peak travel times, increasing gasoline taxes, and offering employees cash or transit vouchers in place of subsidized parking.

State governments could also enact incentives to encourage consumers to buy cleaner, more efficient vehicles. One approach would be to base annual vehicle registration fees on emissions. Another, a "feebate" system, would place a surcharge on gas guzzlers and/or high polluters to finance rebates for the purchase of cars with better fuel efficiency and/or lower emissions.

Proper pricing will also encourage people to get out of their cars altogether, relying on mass transit, walking and cycling to get around. Ultimately, pricing transportation properly could mean that people will move closer to work and school, thus reducing their need to travel.

Oil Spills and Leaks Cause Environmental Disasters

Greenpeace

Greenpeace is an international environmental organization that works to directly confront people and governments that harm the environment.

Oil is harmful to the environment every step of the way. It leaks from pipelines, spills from ships, creates smog in our cities, and is heating up our planet. Marine ecosystems already stressed by overfishing and destructive fishing practices, toxic pollution and climate change are now taking big hits from recent large oil spills.

It also has to be said that while these recent dramatic spills are making the headlines, oil spills actually occur every day. Every year millions of gallons of oil enters the ocean from routine ship and car maintenance, offshore oil drilling operations and ship spills.

Effects of an Oil Spill

While the size of a spill is obviously important, the amount of damage done can depend even more on other factors like the type of oil spilled and the location of the spill—as well as temperature, wind and weather.

Oil can have a smothering effect on marine life, fouling feathers and fur. It is a toxic poison that birds and mammals often ingest while trying to clean themselves. Fish absorb it through direct contact and through their gills. The fumes and contact with oil can also cause nausea and health problems for people in affected areas.

Even when the oil does not kill, it can have more subtle and long-lasting negative effects. For example, it can damage fish eggs, larva and young—wiping out generations. It also can bioaccumulate up through the food chain as predators (including humans) eat numbers of fish (or other wildlife) that have sublethal amounts of oil stored in their bodies. . . .

Cleanup

A rapid and well-resourced response to an oil spill is vitally important. However, it must be acknowledged that a real 'cleanup' in the sense of recovering all the oil and getting the beaches back to normal, is not possible.

Marine ecosystems already stressed by overfishing and destructive fishing practices, toxic pollution and climate change are now taking big hits from recent large oil spills.

Normally to prevent oil from spreading over sea surface they use booms (to contain the oil in polluted areas), and then use skimmers to suck up the oil and pump it into a receiving tank. But the response to oil spills is an extremely difficult and sometimes despairing task.

Booms only work when the waves are small. Even in ideal conditions, with all the equipment and all the experts deployed immediately, recovery of more than 20 percent of the original oil spilled is never practical. Most of it either gets to the shore, or is incorporated into sediments and the seabed, or evaporates.

Once the oil hits the shore, various types of mechanical removal are needed. But some techniques cause damage themselves and, for some very sensitive areas, vigorous cleanup techniques can cause more damage than the oil itself. . . .

Long-term cleanup and support for affected communities is often complicated by a lack of accountability. Often, financial responsibility is limited to the shipowner, while the large multinational oil companies that own the cargo escape responsibility.

However, at least in the case of routine accidents, the oil companies have international regimes that can be called upon to provide financial resources to help, but this is not the case for spills caused by war where often access is difficult due to political problems or the presence of munitions and any financial help is left to donations from governments and non-profit organizations and whatever the UN [United Nations] and others can scrape together.

Even when the oil does not kill, it can have more subtle and long-lasting negative effects.

Recent Spills

Indian Ocean

Source: On 15 August [2006], about 470 km (290 miles) from the coast of India, the Japanese-operated *Bright Artemis* oil tanker collided with a smaller cargo ship it was attempting to assist.

Amount and type: About 5.3 million litres (1.4 million gallons) of crude oil.

Area affected: The spill occurred hundreds of kilometres from land, so substantial impacts on inshore and coastal environments are unlikely.

The effects of 'at sea' spills are less understood than the more obvious effects seen when an oil spill washes up on shore, but could include oiling of offshore seabirds, impacts on marine mammals and turtles and toxicity to organisms occupying surface water layers, including the eggs and larvae of many fish species.

Situation summary: A serious incident, but largely overshadowed by the disastrous spills in the Philippines and Lebanon.

Philippines

Source: *Solar I*, an oil tanker chartered by Petron Corp., the largest oil refiner in the Philippines, sank in rough seas.

Amount and type: About 200,000 litres (53,000 gallons) of bunker oil in the initial spill. The tanker is sunk in deep water, making recovery unlikely and the ship an ecological time bomb with an additional 1.8 million litres (475,000 gallons) of bunker fuel on board.

Area affected: Roughly 320 km (200 miles) of coastline is covered in thick sludge. Miles of coral reef have been destroyed and 1,000 hectares (2,470 acres) of marine reserve badly damaged.

A real 'cleanup' in the sense of recovering all the oil and getting the beaches back to normal, is not possible.

Situation summary: The Philippines' worst oil spill. The government has asked for international assistance to clean up the spill. However, long-term and possible irreversible damage to the environment and livelihoods of people is likely.

As Joseph Gajo, a local marine reserve caretaker, is quoted as saying, "My fear is all the mangrove trees will die. If the mangroves and coral die, this will affect fishermen." According to Guimaras Governor Joaquin Nava, 25,000 people are already affected or displaced.

[A ship owned by the environmental group Greenpeace] . . . is in the area. [It] . . . will assist the Philippines Coast Guard in a visual survey and impact assessment, as well as transport cleanup containment equipment and relief goods donated by the ABS-CBN Foundation and friends of Greenpeace.

Lebanon

Source: On 13 and 15 July 2006, Jieh coastal power station, 28km south of Beirut, was bombed by the Israeli navy. Possibly also oil leaked from an Israeli war frigate [warship] hit by a missile.

Amount and type: Between 11 million and 40 million litres (3–10.5 million gallons; 10,000–15,000 tonnes) of heavy fuel oil has leaked into the sea.

Area affected: Due to winds blowing from the southwest to northeast and water current movement, the oil spill was partly carried out to sea and partly dispersed along the coast. The pollution is estimated to extend at least 150 km (90 miles) offshore, and the oil has hit a 150 km stretch of coastline extending even into Syria.

What is and should be done: Oil needs to be recovered from impacted beaches and from the sea's surface. There are reports and satellite images that show there is some oil offshore, but because aerial surveillance is not currently possible, the amount and extent are not fully known.

In order to get a complete assessment of the extent of the spill, as well as to get equipment and experts to the scene, the air, land and sea blockade needs to be lifted. Oil recovery with safe and secure storage facilities [is] needed, which will help to mitigate the impacts. A full environmental damage assessment programme needs to be implemented.

Greenpeace environmental impact assessment teams in both Israel and Lebanon are helping gather information needed to deal with the environmental cost of the war, including this spill.

Situation summary: This is a significant spill and will have lasting impacts. Heavy fuel oil is persistent in the environment and a significantly large amount of it has washed up onto shore. Containment and cleanup was initially impossible because of the war. These factors make this a particularly nightmarish spill.

Initial coastal cleanup could take 6 to 12 months. The tourism and fishing industries are particularly hard-hit, and one UN spokesperson has been reported as saying the damage could last "up to a century".

How You Can Help

Efficiency and renewable energy can help us reduce our dependence on oil—the only real way to stop oil spills. . . .

Marine reserves strengthen ocean ecosystems—making them better able to withstand and recover from environmental disasters.

Oil and Gas Drilling Operations Have Degraded the Environment of the Western United States

Dusty Horwitt

Dusty Horwitt is a senior analyst for the Environmental Working Group, an environmental organization.

Oil and natural gas companies have drilled almost 120,000 wells in the West since 2000, mostly for natural gas, and nearly 270,000 since 1980, according to industry records analyzed by Environmental Working Group. Yet drilling companies enjoy exemptions under most major federal environmental laws.

Oil and natural gas operations have industrialized the western landscape, punching thousands of wells on pristine lands, injecting toxic chemicals, consuming millions of gallons of water, clawing out pits for their hazardous waste and slashing the ground for sprawling road networks. Every well carries with it the potential for serious environmental degradation.

Federal Environmental Protection Has Dwindled

Yet as drilling has intensified over the past decade, federal environmental protections have dwindled. Unlike most other industries, oil and gas drillers enjoy waivers under the Safe Drinking Water Act, Clean Water Act, Clean Air Act, Resource Conservation and Recovery Act, Superfund, the Emergency Planning and Community Right-to-Know Act and the National Environmental Policy Act.

Companies regularly complain that environmental standards deny them access to drilling sites. But the cratered landscape tells a different story.

Environmental Working Group's analysis of industry records obtained from IHS, an Englewood, Colorado-based energy data company, shows that 99 percent of western oil and gas drilling since 1980 has concentrated in six states: California, Colorado, Montana, New Mexico, Utah and Wyoming. Across the West, 25 counties accounted for 77 percent, or more than 200,000, of the wells drilled since 1980.

As drilling has intensified over the past decade, federal environmental protections have dwindled.

Oil Pollution

The Environmental Protection Agency [EPA] and other government agencies have found that oil and gas drilling is a source of air pollution, a generator of hazardous waste and a potentially huge source of toxic wastewater. As oil and gas drilling proliferates, it presents an exponential threat to the environment, particularly precious western water supplies.

Drilling is likely to explode again when oil and gas prices resume their upward spiral. Before that happens, federal laws must be reformed, with far more stringent standards to prevent pollution from oil and gas drilling operations. Otherwise, millions of acres of western lands and untold surface and underground waters may be irreparably damaged. . . .

Among the key findings [of a report by the Environmental Working Group are the following]:

- The U.S. Bureau of Land Management recently documented toxic benzene contamination in groundwater in Sublette County, Wyoming, where 3,258 wells were drilled between 2000 and 2008. (Just 1,410 wells were drilled there during the previous two decades.) It was not clear what caused the contamination, but benzene is injected underground in hydraulic fracturing, and the extraction process also causes naturally occurring deposits of benzene to surface. Sublette County is rural, making it unlikely that the benzene came from a source other than drilling. Yet Congress and EPA have exempted hydraulic fracturing from the Safe Drinking Water Act that sets standards for underground injection of toxic chemicals.

The Environmental Protection Agency ... [has] found that oil and gas drilling is a source of air pollution, a generator of hazardous waste and a potentially huge source of toxic wastewater.

- Last year, a nurse in LaPlata County, Colorado, almost died from contact with the clothing of a worker she had treated. The worker's clothes were permeated with a chemical fluid used in natural gas drilling. The company that made the fluid refused to identify it, citing trade secrets to the nurse's physician even as he was laboring frantically to save her life. Disclosure is generally required under the federal Emergency Planning and Community Right-to-Know Act, but Congress has exempted the oil and gas industries.

- The New Mexico Oil Conservation Division has identified more than 400 cases statewide of groundwater contamination from oil and gas waste pits. Many of the cases were located in San Juan County, New Mexico, where companies drilled more than 11,000 wells between 1980 and 2008. Yet oil and gas industry wastes are exempted from the federal Resource Conservation and Recovery Act that sets standards for handling of hazardous wastes. In the absence of federal oversight,

New Mexico and Colorado have passed tough new standards designed to minimize pollution from oil and gas drilling, but industry is attempting to roll back these protections. State standards often do not close the loopholes under federal law.

Some members of Congress have proposed closing the oil and gas industry's environmental loopholes. Last year, Reps. Diana DeGette (D-CO [Democrat-Colorado]), Maurice Hinchey (D-NY [Democrat-New York]) and John Salazar (D-CO [Democrat-Colorado]) introduced legislation to repeal the exemption under the Safe Drinking Water Act for hydraulic fracturing, a process pioneered by Halliburton in which oil and gas companies inject toxic chemical-laced water—as many as 6 million gallons per well—to enhance production.

Oil Extraction Threatens the Amazon Rain Forests

Rhett Butler

Rhett Butler is the founder of Mongabay.com, a Web site that aims to raise interest in wildlife and wildlands while promoting awareness of environmental issues.

The extraction of oil is responsible for the deforestation, degradation, and destruction of lands across the globe. The oil extraction process results in the release of toxic drilling by-products into local rivers, while broken pipelines and leakage result in persistent oil spillage. In addition, the construction of roads for accessing remote oil sites opens wild lands to colonists and land developers.

Oil Exploration in Rain Forests

Some of the world's most promising oil and gas deposits lie deep in tropical rain forests. While these fossil fuels can be extracted in an environmentally friendly way, governments and oil companies usually opt for expediency over consideration for the environment or the interests of local people most affected by production.

One of the best known and extreme case studies of oil exploitation in the rain forest is in Ecuador, where the U.S. oil giant Texaco ... seriously degraded an ecosystem over a generation. The firm's oil operations affected the lives of thousands of indigenous peoples and settlers.

The Ecuadorean Oriente, located on the western edge of the Amazon rain forest, is considered the most biodiverse place on Earth. Before Texaco entered in 1967, the region was home to several indigenous groups including the Huaoroni people. Some of these Huaoroni were among the few remaining indigenous peoples on Earth living fully in their traditional ways.

Some of the world's most promising oil and gas deposits lie deep in tropical rain forests.

Over the past three decades, the Oriente has suffered serious degradation and deforestation. Oil spills (green groups allege Texaco dumped more than 20 billion gallons of toxic drilling by-products into local waterways and spilled more than 17 million gallons of crude) and clearing for access roads, exploration, and production activities have damaged the surrounding rain forest and adversely affected the lives of local people. As of the mid-1990s, lands once used for farming lay bare and hundreds of waste pits remained. In August 1992, a pipeline rupture caused a 275,000-gallon (1.04 million L) spill which caused the Rio Napo to run black for days and forced downstream Peru and Brazil to declare national states of emergency for the affected regions.

Originally it appeared that Texaco might pull out of the Oriente without reparations to the people whose environment was so seriously degraded, but widespread protests by indigenous peoples, environmentalists, and human rights organizations forced Texaco into negotiations. Texaco projected its cleanup costs at a moderate US$5–10 million.

In response to the insufficient cleanup gesture, along with widespread environmental degradation and serious health problems among local peoples, a class-action lawsuit was filed against Texaco in the United States on behalf of 30,000 people affected by the oil company's operations. Previous suits against Texaco filed in Ecuador failed due to Texaco's political influence with the Ecuadorean judiciary.

The exploitation of oil in the Ecuadorean Amazon serves as a particularly negative example of oil development projects in the rain forest. Typically, the oil company cuts roads through the forest in order to carry out operations. These roads are followed by transient settlers who colonize and damage the surrounding forest through slash-and-burn agriculture, the introduction of domestic animals, hunting, the collection of fuelwood, and often the introduction of foreign disease to local forest dwellers. Besides the opening of oil roads, oil companies like Texaco burn off by-product natural gas in the open air, a process known as flaring. The flames, besides adding pollutants to the atmosphere, can cause fires that destroy more forest and threaten the lives of locals. In the late 1990s, such gas burning at an Occidental well in Bangladesh was cited as the cause behind a large forest fire.

The oil extraction process can be messy and destructive.

Environmental and Social Costs

The oil extraction process can be messy and destructive. Spills result from burst pipelines and toxic drilling by-products may be dumped directly into local creeks and rivers. Some of the more toxic chemicals are stored in open waste pits and may pollute the surrounding lands and waterways. For security reasons, oil operations may have military involvement.

Oil spills are of tremendous concern in the rain forest. A severe oil spill could have a devastating impact given the variety of river systems—from floating meadows to swamp forest to oxbow lakes to sandbars—that would be affected. The *Exxon Valdez* oil spill was difficult enough to clean up even though it was limited to rocky beaches; addressing a similar-sized spill in the Amazon would be magnitudes more complicated.

Indigenous and local peoples often gain the least from oil extraction, but stand to lose the most. For the impact on their homes, culture, environment, and health, these people generally see little in the form of compensation from the government or oil companies. For example the Ogoni tribesmen in Nigeria have seen little revenue from Shell's activities in the Niger River delta and have mostly relied on sabotage of oil installations to collect oil-spill compensation from Shell. It is meretricious to say oil companies are solely responsible for fleecing locals out of their deserved oil revenues. In many cases, oil companies pay their agreed-upon fees and royalties, which end up in the hands of corrupt government bureaucrats before they can be distributed to the communities. Corruption and oil often go hand in hand.

Despite booming demand for oil and gas, the vast majority of ordinary citizens see little benefit from oil-production activities. In fact, developing countries with large oil reserves have some of the highest debts in the world.

Oil spills are of tremendous concern in the rain forest.

During the 1970s when oil prices were extraordinarily high and real interest rates low, many oil-exporting countries looked much wealthier than they actually were and took out large loans from foreign banks. The loans were used to sponsor costly, often economically inefficient development projects. In the 1980s the creditworthiness of these developing countries collapsed with oil prices, and [sent] the debt of many oil exporters skyrocketing. For example, the national debt of Ecuador has rapidly accelerated since the beginning of the oil boom in the early 1970s. In 1970, the national debt stood at US$256.2 million, but by 2005 the debt had swollen to $16.8 billion.

The sudden inflow of oil can further affect a developing economy by producing a sharp appreciation in the domestic currency which can make non-oil sectors like agriculture and manufacturing less competitive on world markets, thus leaving oil to dominate the economy. The country then becomes vulnerable to wild price swings in the commodity market.

Over-reliance on oil can also impact the government's responsiveness to its citizens. Michael [L.] Ross, an associate professor of political science at the University of California, Los Angeles, believes that oil-rich countries do less to help their poor than do countries without oil and are plagued with lower literacy rates, score lower on measures like the UN's [United Nations'] Human Development Index, and have higher child mortality and malnutrition. How is this possible? The *Economist* explains, "Unlike agriculture, the oil sector employs few unskilled people. The inherent volatility of commodity prices hurts the poor the most, as they are least able to hedge their risks. And because the resource is concentrated, the resulting wealth passes through only a few hands—and so is more susceptible to misdirection." Since oil revenues are sometimes funneled directly to rulers, governments have little need to raise revenues through taxes and be accountable to their citizens.

Political and economic considerations aside, oil conglomerates are easy targets for environmentalists. Their operations are highly conspicuous and create a dramatic impact on the local economy and the local social conditions. Since local communities reap few benefits from oil development, while shouldering the bulk of the social and environmental costs, it is easy to see why the contribution of oil development to environmental devastation is often overstated.

Increasing Demand for Fossil Fuels Will Cause Even Greater Environmental Damage in the Future

Agence France-Presse (AFP)

Agence France-Presse (AFP) is a news agency based in Paris, France.

The world's dependence on fossil fuels, particularly coal, is set to rocket over the next two decades, with China and India leading demand, the International Energy Agency [IEA] has warned.

The IEA, energy watchdog and advisor to 26 countries, on Wednesday [November 2007] published a bleak picture of energy demand in its *World Energy Outlook 2007* report, a study which highlights long-term trends that will shape energy policy up to 2030.

Coal will make a comeback, the Middle East and Russia will grow in influence as oil suppliers, and emerging giants China and India will account for most of the increase in energy demand.

"The trends in energy demand, imports, coal use and greenhouse gas emissions to 2030 in this year's *World Energy Outlook* [WEO] are even worse than projected in WEO 2006," the agency warned.

It gave little hope to those looking for a technological breakthrough, which many believe is necessary for a meaningful reduction in world greenhouse gas emissions.

The Paris-based research centre did not identify a clean, new source of energy that can provide the power needed to fuel improvements in living conditions for the world's poor without damaging the environment.

Coal as King

Instead, it predicted that coal, one of the oldest and dirtiest sources of energy, would be king in emerging countries China and India in 2030.

Coal, one of the oldest and dirtiest sources of energy, [could] . . . be king in emerging countries China and India in 2030.

"In line with its spectacular growth over the past few years, coal sees the biggest increase in demand in absolute terms, jumping by 73 percent between 2005 and 2030," the agency said.

"China and India, which already account for 45 percent of world coal use, drive over four-fifths of the increase (in its use) to 2030."

The 663-page report was packed with alarming statistics based on a "reference scenario" in which energy consumption continues on current trends without government measures to reduce demand and greenhouse gas emissions.

Under this model, energy demand increases by more than 50 percent up to 2030, with 84 percent of the new demand supplied from fossil fuels.

China and India's energy needs, measured in tonnes of oil equivalent, more than double from 2005–2030. China's energy demand surpasses that of the US [United States] after 2010 and its pollution problems worsen.

China is also set to become the world's biggest emitter of greenhouse gas emissions this year, the IEA said.

Coal-fired power stations have been "the primary cause of the surge in global emissions in the last few years," the IEA said, and new power stations in China and India are likely to be mostly coal-fired.

Energy demand increases by more than 50 percent up to 2030, with 84 percent of the new demand supplied from fossil fuels.

China is set to build new power stations with output of more than the installed capacity of the United States. India needs as much as the installed capacity of Japan, South Korea and Australia combined, the report found.

Reducing Carbon Emissions

Because of this, the IEA urged governments to focus on developing clean coal technologies, in particular carbon capture and sequestration (CCS), which entails capturing carbon and storing it underground.

According to its calculations, if governments do not take further action, the world's temperature could rise by six degrees centigrade beyond 2030, Fatih Birol, head of research at the IEA, told AFP [Agence France-Presse].

The report also included two other scenarios; one entitled "alternative policy" in which governments enact measures (which are currently under discussion) to increase energy efficiency and reduce greenhouse gas emissions.

And another "high-growth policy" in which the Indian and Chinese economies grow faster than the "conservative" rate of 6.0 percent per annum used in the other two scenarios.

Even under the "alternative" model, carbon dioxide emissions in 2030 are still more than 25 percent higher than now, and the "high-growth" model is even worse.

A bigger reduction in emissions requires policy action and technological transformation "on an unprecedented scale," the IEA said.

Higher Oil Prices

The conclusions of the IEA are also of vital importance for international relations.

If governments do not take further action, the world's temperature could rise by six degrees centigrade beyond 2030.

The grip of Middle Eastern producers and Russia on world oil resources will tighten, although the IEA did say that there was sufficient oil to satisfy demand so long as planned investments in new capacity are made.

The 12-member Organization of [the] Petroleum Exporting Countries, which is dominated by Saudi Arabia, is projected to provide 52 percent of world [oil] supply in 2030, up from 42 percent presently.

"The greater the increase in call on oil and gas from these regions, the more likely it will be that they will seek to extract a higher rent from their exports and to impose higher prices in the longer term," the IEA said.

This is bad news for consuming countries with oil prices already at nearly 100 dollars per barrel.

Peak Oil Could Have Disastrous Effects on the Environment

Grinning Planet

Grinning Planet is an environmental Web site.

It might be tempting to think that burning less petroleum-based fuel in the future will reduce pollution. After all, there would be fewer tailpipe emissions from vehicles, fewer jets painting the sky with pollution, fewer motorboats and Jet Skis leaking fuel into bays and rivers, and fewer snowmobiles making a smoky racket in our national parks and elsewhere.

Some peak oil analysts also deemphasize the threat from global climate change, asserting that the reduced burning of petroleum-based fuels in planes, trucks, cars, and other vehicles will reduce carbon emissions enough that we should forget about global warming and start spending all of our time worrying about peak oil. Indeed, in 2008, spiking oil prices and the beginning of the ever-worsening economic depression combined to reduce US CO_2 emissions by 2.8% in 2008. Total global CO_2 emissions, however, increased by 1.7%, and that's what counts.

Petroleum is the basic ingredient in plastics, pesticides, and chemicals—all of which are overused and misused, and are serious problems for the environment (and the people and creatures that live in it). Less of those things would be a positive, environmentally.

So, generally speaking, will less available oil will mean less pollution from petroleum-based products? Will peak oil have a positive impact on the environment? In the long term, it probably will. Unfortunately, in the near term, peak oil promises to have a devastating impact on the environment on a number of fronts. Let's go through some examples.

Non-Conventional Oil

The petroleum industry has a number of quality gradations for oil sources, but for our purposes, we can simply divide the sources for petroleum products into two categories:

- *conventional oil,* which includes "light crude" and other crude oils that are relatively easy to extract and refine; and

- *non-conventional oil,* which includes the heaviest liquid oils as well as the Athabasca oil sands in Canada, "Orinoco belt" bitumen in oil-rich Venezuela, and oil shale deposits in the western US.

Deposits of non-conventional petroleum sources are vast—much greater than the remaining deposits of conventional oils. There are two problems, though:

1. These sources are hard to mine and refine.
2. Their net "energy returned on energy invested" (EROEI) is not nearly as good as the EROEI for conventional sources. Their EROEI will decline even further if they are subject to "carbon capture" schemes.

The first problem directly translates into more pollution and environmental damage due to the methods that have to be used. The second also means more pollution at current rates of energy consumption, since more pollution is produced per unit of energy available.

Most petroleum analysts agree that conventional oil has already peaked and that total oil production levels have been kept stable by increasing production from unconventional sources. As the decline in conventional oil accelerates, there will be evermore pressure to exploit non-conventional sources, many of which were previously non-viable, either for economic reasons or because their extraction would cause too much environmental damage. Skyrocketing oil prices will take care of the economic impediments for most non-conventional oil sources. It also seems probable that public resistance to dirty production processes will wither as fuel becomes more expensive, shortages test our .patience, and the economic impact of tighter, more expensive energy supplies takes us into leaner times.

As the decline in conventional oil accelerates, there will be evermore pressure to exploit non-conventional sources, many of which . . . cause too much environmental damage.

Deepwater Oil

At the dawn of the oil age, we were drilling for oil only on land. Then, as we realized that areas offshore (but not too far offshore) also had oil and gas deposits—and that we could extract those resources—we started drilling there too. That was more expensive than drilling on land, but as long as the price of oil made it economically feasible—and as long as environmental problems could be sidestepped—we drilled, extracted, and produced.

The next logical step is deepwater oil—further offshore and in much deeper water. Indeed, there is oil in such places, and production of deepwater oil is now at a few million barrels per day (about 4% of total production).

There is more deepwater oil to be found and extracted, for sure, but deepwater oil has some technical, logistical, and environmental challenges:

- Insufficient numbers of capable oil rigs.

- Separating and dealing with the gas and water that come up with the deepwater oil.

- Transporting deepwater oil and gas.

- Dealing with deepwater accidents.

There is more deepwater oil to be found and extracted, for sure, but deepwater oil has some technical, logistical, and environmental challenges.

Despite these challenges, deepwater oil production is expected to double by the middle of the 2010s. Of course, such an increase is less than the overall rate of depletion from existing oil sources, but it's still a help. Remember, though, that the more extraordinary the effort required to extract, transport, and refine any source of oil, the less net energy you get from that oil source, and the more pollution you generate per BTU.

Coal

Many energy analysts correctly point out that coal, despite its dirty nature, is likely to be a primary energy source for the world for decades to come:

- There is lots of it, notably in the US and China, which are both big energy users and big importers of oil.

- The technologies and infrastructure needed to utilize coal are well established.

Most of the coal today is used for electricity production, so what does that have to do with tightening oil supplies? There are two ways a scarcity of liquid fuels could increase demand for coal:

- *Coal to liquids (CTL) for direct fuel substitution*—Coal can be converted to a synthetic fuel that can be used like diesel or jet fuel.

- *Electricity to power plug-in hybrids*—The emergence of plug-in hybrids will be a natural follow-on to the success of gas-electric hybrids. Such vehicles would indeed be very efficient, but we will need more electricity to feed them.

Each of these methods has environmental drawbacks. . . .

Coal, despite its dirty nature, is likely to be a primary energy source for the world for decades to come.

Biofuels

First, let's define the two main categories of biofuels:

- *Liquid fuels*—typically ethanol or biodiesel, usually derived from plant materials like corn, sugarcane, soybeans (soya), or palm oil.

- *Biomass*—firewood, brush, crop residue, and any other plant material that can be burned directly as fuel.

From some aspects, biofuels are a good thing. For instance:

- Petroleum reserves will run out one day (or, more properly, what remains will be uneconomical to extract and refine). The crops we need to make biofuels, on the other hand, can be grown year after year after year.

- Because crops are replanted every year and reabsorb the CO_2 that was emitted when the previous year's biofuels supply was burned, the fuels are in theory carbon-neutral. (In practice, ethanol production uses non-biofuel energy, tarnishing its good greenhouse-gas balance.)

- Overall, ethanol is cleaner-burning than gasoline, and biodiesel is cleaner-burning than regular diesel.

But the environmental impact of moving from petroleum-based fuels to biofuels deserves close scrutiny.

You won't be seeing organic or biodynamically grown crops being used to feed ethanol and biodiesel processing plants any time soon. It will be standard crops, and that means the standard problems of industrial agriculture apply:

- It's chemically intensive and highly polluting (i.e., lots of troublesome pesticides and fertilizers).

- The corn and soybeans grown are typically genetically engineered, which means more chemical herbicide use and risks to the viability of organic farming because of overuse of the organic insecticide Bt in Bt corn.

- Huge parcels of rain forest were already being cut down so soybeans could be planted to supply feedlots. Now, more of this will happen so that additional soybean farms and palm plantations can be established to keep up with demand from the biodiesel industry.

More of these crops means more impact from unsustainable farming practices—local air and water pollution, more chemicals in the environment and in us, more coastal dead zones. Increasing demand for ethanol and biodiesel will also mean more marginal farmland will be put into crops rather than letting it stay fallow, resulting in more soil erosion and more water pollution due to loss of riparian (streamside) buffer zones.

Ethanol production has a barely positive EROEI—the energy available in the corn kernels just doesn't give you that much more energy in your tank than you put into the overall process, if you include farming, transport, and processing. Ethanol defenders are quick to point to the greater potential of "cellulosic" ethanol, where the whole plant can be used to feed the ethanol production process. True enough—if the nascent technology can be made production-worthy. But even then there would be a serious sustainability problem: Standard farming practices—those that give us the corn and other feedstocks—lead to nutrient depletion over time. Cellulosic ethanol practices will cause much quicker nutrient depletion since the crop residue is not being returned to the soil to feed the organisms that make soil.

The same goes for biomass that is burned. Taking whole plants from the farm fields, prairies, or forests and returning nothing will, over time, degrade the soil faster than natural processes can replenish it, and the yields will fall to the point that the EROEI is negative. . . .

Some production of biofuels is inevitable and even beneficial. But a massive increase in crop production for liquid biofuels or harvesting of prairie and forest plants for burning or cellulosic ethanol production will not work in the long term due to soil fertility limitations. Boosters of biofuels understand plenty about energy but little about soil, and diving deep into this pool is a recipe for environmental disaster. Doing so will also divert precious resources from energy solutions that do have a chance of long-term success.

Nuclear Energy

Once plug-in hybrids hit the market, demand for electricity will start to rise even faster than it already is. Nuclear energy supporters see this as an opportunity to promote their product.

Whether you believe the industry's claims that nuclear is a "clean" technology, what is indisputable is that nuclear waste is a problem that has no known solution. Even if the Yucca Mountain facility ever comes online—which it may not due to growing technical concerns—it will already be 3/4 full with just the spent fuel that now needs a final resting place. Greatly increasing the number of nuclear plants in the US and the world—whether under the guise of combating global warming or meeting rising electricity demand—would mean that *multiple* Yucca-type facilities would be needed.

Nuclear energy also makes little economic sense if "externalities" like fuel production and waste management are included. The fact that the US government had to pass a multibillion-dollar incentive package before any private entity would consider a new nuclear plant shows what an economic loser nuclear is.

The nuclear industry has powerful friends, has good-sounding (if specious) sales pitches, and unarguably can produce needed power. So, we may go down this road. But a resurgence of nuclear power is probably the worst way in which we can "go dirty before we go dark"—not only will we create more highly toxic pollution for our own environment, that pollution will last for hundreds of generations to come. . . .

Methane Hydrates

Deep in the oceans, there are vast deposits of methane (natural gas) trapped in the form of hydrates. The problem is how to extract these hydrates economically. In terms of environmental impact, the potential for such extractions to release some of the methane, a potent greenhouse gas, into the air seems rather high.

The logistical difficulty of this energy source makes it an unlikely candidate for the future. . . .

The environmental impact of moving from petroleum-based fuels to biofuels deserves close scrutiny.

Hydrogen

First, here on Earth, hydrogen is an energy carrier, not a fuel. Second, the technological challenges associated with hydrogen—for production, logistics, and efficient use—are daunting. Third, the only reasonably efficient way to make hydrogen today is from fossil fuels—typically natural gas—but that is still less efficient overall for delivering energy than just burning the fossil fuels themselves for energy.

If hydrogen's problems can be worked out, we'll cheer. But it will take decades, if it happens at all, and by then the problems of peak oil will have demanded more immediate solutions. . . .

The Chaos Factor

At this point, we've covered most of the solutions that would normally be thought of as having the best scalability and/or direct applicability to the coming liquid fuels crisis. Unfortunately, we've also shown that each of them has serious environmental repercussions, even if current environmental regulations are applied. But it gets worse. Enter the "Chaos Factor."

Whether you believe the industry's claims that nuclear is a "clean" technology, . . . what is indisputable is that nuclear waste is a problem that has no known solution.

Free-trade promoters are quick to point out that economic prosperity is the best way to improve the environment; thus, we should be promoting more WTO-style [World Trade Organization-style] trade with developing nations, not less. To some extent, their argument is specious—the prosperous West has solved much of its environmental problem by exporting the polluting processes to developing countries, and we are largely stalled in our efforts to make progress on the remaining pollution problems at home and around the world. But the free-traders' assertion is correct to the extent that only in a prosperous society is the standard of living far enough above subsistence level to allow widespread support for accepting even the relatively minor economic costs associated with curbing pollution.

Now, let's take a step forward in time with the Ghost of Peak Oil Future. Oil is over $200 per barrel and gasoline is $9.50 a gallon. The US economy is in a severe depression, partly due to the drag on productivity caused by expensive oil, but more so from the blow that occurred when the country's unsustainable debt bubble (federal and personal) finally burst and foreign bond holders cashed in their chips. Unemployment in the US is 35%, and those with jobs are working for far less than they used to. Millions more families have lost their homes. Disruption of agricultural supply chains, inflation in the money system, and widespread hoarding leave grocery store shelves bare on a regular basis. Basic services such as electricity, roads, water, and telephones are starting to degrade due to lack of maintenance in the economically constrained times. In short, most are in survival mode.

Environmental regulations will be "eased," "reformed" and "streamlined"—which is environmental doublespeak for "gutted."

In such circumstances, people are not likely to have much time to worry about keeping the environment clean, and there will be little political support for eco-issues. Worse, right-wingers will seize the opportunity to attack environmentalists, asserting that "eco-maniacs" caused the problem in the first place with "extreme regulations." That is actually the opposite of the truth—if our leaders had been listening to progressives' warnings about oil dependence and unsustainable energy addictions . . . the disaster might have been avoided. But the corporate media will likely see "it's the environmentalists' fault" as an easy story to sell to an angry, desperate public.

Will it really be that bleak? We hope not. But if we take even a few steps in the direction of bleakitude, it seems likely that all of the "solutions" discussed in the previous sections of this article will be pursued—and more. Environmental regulations will be "eased," "reformed" and "streamlined"—which is environmental doublespeak for "gutted"—and drilling, mining, refining, burning, nuking, and all other energy-related activities will proceed full-speed-ahead.

So, we see that peak oil and overall energy constraints have a lot of non-solutions—or at least solutions whose environmental impact is unpalatable.

CHAPTER 3

Is the World Running Out of Oil?

Chapter Preface

One of the most controversial topics involving the subject of oil resources is whether world oil production has peaked—that is, whether humans have used up about half of global oil reserves, so that oil production has reached its peak, leading to a slow decline in the future. This idea of peak oil does not mean that the world will run out of oil soon, but it could mean the end of cheap oil and the start of an oil market that requires producers to look for lesser-quality oil or oil found in locations that are difficult and expensive to develop, such as under deep ocean waters. Eventually, the expense of extracting the oil may be more than the oil is worth, and at that point, oil production could come to a halt. The concept of peak oil is not new, however; it dates back to the 1950s, when U.S. geologist M. King Hubbert became the first to predict an oil peak.

Marion King Hubbert (1903–1989) was a scholar with bachelor's, master's, and doctorate degrees from the University of Chicago, where he studied geology, physics, and mathematics. He spent much of his professional career working for Shell Oil Company and Shell Development Company in Houston, Texas—as a research geophysicist, then as associate director of exploration and production research, and later as chief consultant in general geology. In 1963 Hubbert left Shell to take jobs as a research geologist with the U.S. Geological Survey and as a professor of geology and geophysics at Stanford University in California. He also taught for a time at the University of California, Berkeley. In 1976 Hubbert retired from academia, but he continued his relationship with the U.S. Geological Survey.

Hubbert first attracted public attention in 1949 shortly after he joined Shell Oil Company. At a time when the United

States was still a major oil producer and the world's resources seemed limitless, he publicly predicted that the fossil fuel era would not last long. In 1956, in spite of pressure to remain silent from Shell, Hubbert presented a paper to the American Petroleum Institute in San Antonio, Texas, that predicted oil production in the United States would peak between 1965 and 1970, then decline as reserves dried up. He offered mathematical proof for his theory—a bell-shaped curve that later became known as Hubbert's curve or Hubbert's peak. According to Hubbert's theory, the production rate of not only oil, but also of any finite natural resource, will follow a roughly symmetrical bell-shaped curve in which production increases rapidly from the time of discovery until it hits a peak, at which point it will begin a steep decline.

Hubbert's prediction startled the oil industry and drew much criticism from skeptical observers who could not imagine the United States running out of oil. Hubbert urged the U.S. government to prepare for the coming oil shortages by importing and storing foreign oil, but his recommendations were ignored. His warnings were forgotten as the United States continued enjoying its oil glut and became known as the automobile capital of the world. Hubbert became famous a couple of decades later, however, when his 1956 prediction proved correct. In 1970, American oil production reached its highest historical level—and then began dropping. Hubbert's theory on oil depletion was officially acknowledged in 1975 by the National Academy of Sciences, a society of distinguished scholars who advise the federal government about science and technology matters. The peaking of U.S. oil marked a new era for the United States. The country was forced to import more and more of its oil, ultimately making it dangerously dependent on foreign sources. This, in turn, led to a growing U.S. strategic interest in befriending or otherwise controlling foreign countries with large oil deposits and ensuring the free flow of oil to the West.

In 1973, when the United States was importing approximately 40 percent of its oil, the U.S. vulnerability to foreign oil producers was made abundantly clear when a group of oil-producing countries in the Middle East—the Organization of Arab Petroleum Exporting Countries (OAPEC)—announced an oil embargo against the United States and other industrialized countries in response to America's decision to supply the Israeli military with weapons during the Arab-Israeli War. The embargo caused the price of oil to almost quadruple, created gasoline shortages that forced consumers to wait in long lines at gas stations, and wreaked havoc on the U.S. economy, which soon experienced a period of high inflation. The embargo was lifted in 1974, but high oil prices and other economic effects lingered, as did the U.S. reliance on imported oil. By 2000, the United States was importing more oil than it was exporting, and today, based on the latest figures from the U.S. Department of Energy's Energy Information Administration (EIA), the United States imports almost 70 percent of its oil.

Later in his life, Hubbert predicted that global oil production would peak between 1995 and 2000. The Arab oil embargo helped to dampen demand, however, and probably extended the date of global peak oil. Many experts today speculate that the actual date of global peak oil production has either already passed or is coming in the very near future. They worry that the oil supply may decline just at the time when the world is experiencing ever larger demands for oil due to rapid economic development in countries such as China and India. Others, however, are less concerned, believing that new oil development will keep pace with demand or that rising oil prices will lead to technological discoveries of alternative energy sources. The viewpoints in this chapter debate the issues of whether global oil production is peaking and whether the world will run out of oil.

The World Oil Supply Is Running Out Fast

Steve Connor

Steve Connor is the science editor for the Independent, *a British newspaper.*

The world is heading for a catastrophic energy crunch that could cripple a global economic recovery because most of the major oil fields in the world have passed their peak production, a leading energy economist has warned.

Higher oil prices brought on by a rapid increase in demand and a stagnation, or even decline, in supply could blow any recovery off course, said Dr Fatih Birol, the chief economist at the respected International Energy Agency (IEA) in Paris, which is charged with the task of assessing future energy supplies by OECD [Organisation for Economic Co-operation and Development] countries.

Faster than Predicted

In an interview with the *Independent*, Dr Birol said that the public and many governments appeared to be oblivious to the fact that the oil on which modern civilisation depends is running out far faster than previously predicted and that global production is likely to peak in about 10 years—at least a decade earlier than most governments had estimated.

But the first detailed assessment of more than 800 oil fields in the world, covering three-quarters of global reserves, has found that most of the biggest fields have already peaked and that the rate of decline in oil production is now running at nearly twice the pace as calculated just two years ago. On top of this, there is a problem of chronic underinvestment by oil-producing countries, a feature that is set to result in an "oil crunch" within the next five years which will jeopardise any hope of a recovery from the present global economic recession, he said.

The first detailed assessment of more than 800 oil fields in the world, covering three-quarters of global reserves, has found that most of the biggest fields have already peaked.

In a stark warning to Britain and the other Western powers, Dr Birol said that the market power of the very few oil-producing countries that hold substantial reserves of oil—mostly in the Middle East—would increase rapidly as the oil crisis begins to grip after 2010.

"One day we will run out of oil, it is not today or tomorrow, but one day we will run out of oil and we have to leave oil before oil leaves us, and we have to prepare ourselves for that day," Dr Birol said. "The earlier we start, the better, because all of our economic and social system is based on oil, so to change from that will take a lot of time and a lot of money and we should take this issue very seriously," he said.

"The market power of the very few oil-producing countries, mainly in the Middle East, will increase very quickly. They already have about 40 percent share of the oil market and this will increase much more strongly in the future," he said.

There is now a real risk of a crunch in the oil supply after next year [2010] when demand picks up because not enough is being done to build up new supplies of oil to compensate for the rapid decline in existing fields.

The IEA estimates that the decline in oil production in existing fields is now running at 6.7 percent a year compared to the 3.7 percent decline it had estimated in 2007, which it now acknowledges to be wrong.

"If we see a tightness of the markets, people in the street will see it in terms of higher prices, much higher than we see now. It will have an impact on the economy, definitely, especially if we see this tightness in the markets in the next few years," Dr Birol said.

"It will be especially important because the global economy will still be very fragile, very vulnerable. Many people think there will be a recovery in a few years' time but it will be a slow recovery and a fragile recovery and we will have the risk that the recovery will be strangled with higher oil prices," he told the *Independent*.

There is now a real risk of a crunch in the oil supply after next year [2010] when demand picks up because not enough is being done to build up new supplies of oil.

Unsustainable Consumption

In its first-ever assessment of the world's major oil fields, the IEA concluded that the global energy system was at a crossroads and that consumption of oil was "patently unsustainable", with expected demand far outstripping supply.

Oil production has already peaked in non-OPEC [Organization of the Petroleum Exporting Countries] countries and the era of cheap oil has come to an end, it warned.

In most fields, oil production has now peaked, which means that other sources of supply have to be found to meet existing demand.

Even if demand remained steady, the world would have to find the equivalent of four Saudi Arabias to maintain production, and six Saudi Arabias if it is to keep up with the expected increase in demand between now and 2030, Dr Birol said.

"It's a big challenge in terms of the geology, in terms of the investment and in terms of the geopolitics. So this is a big risk and it's mainly because of the rates of the declining oil fields," he said.

"Many governments now are more and more aware that at least the day of cheap and easy oil is over ... [however] I'm not very optimistic about governments being aware of the difficulties we may face in the oil supply," he said.

Environmentalists fear that as supplies of conventional oil run out, governments will be forced to exploit even dirtier alternatives, such as the massive reserves of tar sands in Alberta, Canada, which would be immensely damaging to the environment because of the amount of energy needed to recover a barrel of tar sand oil compared to the energy needed to collect the same amount of crude oil.

Environmentalists fear that as supplies of conventional oil run out, governments will be forced to exploit even dirtier alternatives.

"Just because oil is running out faster than we have collectively assumed, does not mean the pressure is off on climate change," said Jeremy Leggett, a former oil-industry consultant and now a green entrepreneur with Solar Century.

"Shell and others want to turn to tar, and extract oil from coal. But these are very carbon-intensive processes, and will deepen the climate problem," Dr Leggett said.

"What we need to do is accelerate the mobilisation of renewables, energy efficiency and alternative transport.

"We have to do this for global warming reasons anyway, but the imminent energy crisis redoubles the imperative," he said.

Oil: An Unclear Future

•*Why is oil so important as an energy source?*

Crude oil has been critical for economic development and the smooth functioning of almost every aspect of society. Agriculture and food production [are] heavily dependent on oil for fuel and fertilisers. In the US [United States], for instance, it takes the direct and indirect use of about six barrels of oil to raise one beef steer. It is the basis of most transport systems. Oil is also crucial to the drugs and chemicals industries and is a strategic asset for the military.

•How are oil reserves estimated?

The amount of oil recoverable is always going to be an assessment subject to the vagaries of economics—which determines the price of the oil and whether it is worth the costs of pumping it out—and technology, which determines how easy it is to discover and recover. Probable reserves have a better than 50 percent chance of getting oil out. Possible reserves have less than 50 percent chance.

•Why is there such disagreement over oil reserves?

All numbers tend to be informed estimates. Different experts make different assumptions so it is understandable that they can come to different conclusions. Some countries see the size of their oil fields as a national security issue and do not want to provide accurate information. Another problem concerns how fast oil production is declining in fields that are past their peak production. The rate of decline can vary from field to field and this affects calculations on the size of the reserves. A further factor is the expected size of future demand for oil.

•What is "peak oil" and when will it be reached?

This is the point when the maximum rate at which oil is extracted reaches a peak because of technical and geological constraints, with global production going into decline from then on. The UK [United Kingdom] government, along with many other governments, has believed that peak oil will not occur until well into the 21st century, at least not until after 2030. The International Energy Agency believes peak oil will come perhaps by 2020. But it also believes that we are heading for an even earlier "oil crunch" because demand after 2010 is likely to exceed dwindling supplies.

•*With global warming, why should we be worried about peak oil?*

There are large reserves of non-conventional oil, such as the tar sands of Canada. But this oil is dirty and will produce vast amounts of carbon dioxide which will make . . . nonsense of any climate change agreement. Another problem concerns how fast oil production is declining in fields that are past their peak production. The rate of decline can vary from field to field and this affects calculations on the size of the reserves. If we are not adequately prepared for peak oil, global warming could become far worse than expected.

Peak Oil Occurred on a Worldwide Basis in 2008

Richard Heinberg

Richard Heinberg is an American author, a journalist, and an educator, who has written extensively about ecological issues.

On July 11, 2008, the price of a barrel of oil hit a record $147.27 in daily trading. That same month, world crude oil production achieved a record 74.8 million barrels per day.

For years prior to this, a growing legion of analysts had been arguing that world oil production would max out around the year 2010 and begin to decline for reasons having to do with geology (we have found and picked the world's "low-hanging fruit" in terms of giant oil fields), as well as lack of drilling rigs and trained exploration geologists and engineers. "Peak Oil," they insisted, would mark the end of the growth phase of industrial civilization, because economic expansion requires increasing amounts of high-quality energy.

Peak Oil in 2008

During the period from 2005 to 2008, as oil's price steadily rose, production remained stagnant. Though new sources of oil were coming online, they barely made up for production declines in existing fields due to depletion. By mid-2008, as oil prices wafted to the stratosphere, every petroleum producer responded to the obvious incentive to pump every possible barrel. Production rates nudged upward for a couple of months, but then both prices and production fell as demand for oil collapsed.

Since then, with oil prices much lower, and with credit tight to unavailable, up to $150 billion of investments in the

Richard Heinberg, "Peak Oil Day," *MuseLetter*, no. 207, July 2009. http://richard heinberg.com. Reproduced by permission development of future petroleum production capacity have evaporated. This means that if a new record production level is to be achieved, further declines in production from existing fields have to be overcome, meaning that all of those canceled production projects, and many more in addition, will have to be quickly brought onstream. It may not be physically possible to turn the tide at this point, given the fact that the new "plays" are technically demanding and therefore expensive to develop, and have limited productive potential.

On May 4 of this year [2009], Raymond James [&] Associates, a prominent brokerage specializing in energy investments, issued a report stating, "With OPEC [Organization of the Petroleum Exporting Countries] oil production apparently having peaked in 1Q08, and non-OPEC even earlier in 2007, peak oil on a worldwide basis seems to have taken place in early 2008." This conclusion is being echoed by a cadre of other analysts.

During the period from 2005 to 2008, as oil's price steadily rose, production remained stagnant.

Maybe it's a stretch to say that the production peak occurred at one identifiable moment, but attributing it to the day oil prices reached their high-water mark may be a useful way of fixing the event in our minds. So I suggest that we remember July 11, 2008, as Peak Oil Day.

We are now approaching the first-year anniversary of Peak Oil Day. Where are we now? The global economy is in tatters, yet oil prices have recovered somewhat (they're now about half what they were in July 2008). World energy consumption is down, world trade is down, the airline industry is shrinking, and most of the world's automakers are on life support.

Adapting to Less Oil

It is too late to prepare for Peak Oil—a year too late, in fact. Now the name of the game is adaptation. We are in an entirely new economic environment, in which old assumptions about the inevitability of perpetual growth, and the usefulness of leveraging investments based on expectations of future growth, are crashing in flames. Even if economic activity picks up somewhat, this will occur in the context of an economy significantly smaller than the one that existed in July 2008, and energy scarcity will quickly cause most green shoots to wither.

It is impossible to say what will happen in the future with regard to oil prices. Clearly, very high prices kill demand by undercutting economic activity. Thus it is possible that the barrel price of petroleum may never break last year's record. On the other hand, if the value of the dollar were to collapse, then the sky's the limit for prices in dollars per barrel.

It is easier to forecast the oil supply trend: Though we'll see level-to-rising production temporarily from time to time, in general it's down, down, downhill from now on.

Even though Peak Oil is now in the past, its annual commemoration on Peak Oil Day may serve an important purpose by reminding us why our economy is shrinking, and by focusing our thoughts on ways to facilitate the transition to a post-petroleum world.

The U.S. Government Predicts a Sharp Drop in World Oil Output

Michael T. Klare

Michael T. Klare is a professor of peace and world security studies at Hampshire College in Amherst, Massachusetts, and the author of Rising Powers, Shrinking Planet: The New Geopolitics of Energy.

Every summer, the Energy Information Administration (EIA) of the U.S. Department of Energy issues its *International Energy Outlook* (IEO)—a jam-packed compendium of data and analysis on the evolving world energy equation. For those with the background to interpret its key statistical findings, the release of the IEO can provide a unique opportunity to gauge important shifts in global energy trends, much as reports of routine Communist Party functions in the party journal *Pravda* once provided America's Kremlin watchers with insights into changes in the Soviet Union's top leadership circle.

As it happens, the recent release of the 2009 IEO has provided energy watchers with a feast of significant revelations. By far the most significant disclosure: The IEO predicts a sharp drop in projected future world oil output (compared to previous expectations) and a corresponding increase in reliance on what are called "unconventional fuels"—oil sands, ultra-deep oil, shale oil, and biofuels.

So here's the headline for you: For the first time, the well-respected Energy Information Administration appears to be joining with those experts who have long argued that the era of cheap and plentiful oil is drawing to a close. Almost as notable, when it comes to news, the 2009 report highlights Asia's insatiable demand for energy and suggests that China is moving ever closer to the point at which it will overtake the United States as the world's number one energy consumer. Clearly, a new era of cutthroat energy competition is upon us.

Peak Oil Becomes the New Norm

As recently as 2007, the IEO projected that the global production of conventional oil (the stuff that comes gushing out of the ground in liquid form) would reach 107.2 million barrels per day in 2030, a substantial increase from the 81.5 million barrels produced in 2006. Now, in 2009, the latest edition of the report has grimly dropped that projected 2030 figure to just 93.1 million barrels per day—in future-output terms, an eye-popping decline of 14.1 million expected barrels per day.

> *The well-respected Energy Information Administration appears to be joining with those experts who have long argued that the era of cheap and plentiful oil is drawing to a close.*

Even when you add in the 2009 report's projection of a larger increase than once expected in the output of unconventional fuels, you still end up with a net projected decline of 11.1 million barrels per day in the global supply of liquid fuels (when compared to the IEO's soaring 2007 projected figures). What does this decline signify—other than growing pessimism by energy experts when it comes to the international supply of petroleum liquids?

Very simply, it indicates that the usually optimistic analysts at the Department of Energy now believe global fuel supplies will simply not be able to keep pace with rising world energy demands. For years now, assorted petroleum geologists and other energy types have been warning that world oil output is approaching a maximum sustainable daily level—a peak—and will subsequently go into decline, possibly producing global economic chaos. Whatever the timing of the arrival of peak oil's actual peak, there is growing agreement that we have, at last, made it into peak-oil territory, if not yet to the moment of irreversible decline.

Until recently, Energy Information Administration officials scoffed at the notion that a peak in global oil output was imminent or that we should anticipate a contraction in the future availability of petroleum anytime soon. "[We] expect conventional oil to peak closer to the middle than to the beginning of the 21st century," the 2004 IEO report stated emphatically.

Consistent with this view, the EIA reported one year later that global production would reach a staggering 122.2 million barrels per day in 2025, more than 50% above the 2002 level of 80.0 million barrels per day. This was about as close to an explicit rejection of peak oil that you could get from the EIA's experts.

Where Did All the Oil Go?

Now, let's turn back to the 2009 edition. In 2025, according to this new report, world liquids output, conventional and unconventional, will reach only a relatively dismal 101.1 million barrels per day. Worse yet, conventional oil output will be just 89.6 million barrels per day. In EIA terms, this is pure gloom and doom, about as deeply pessimistic when it comes to the world's future oil output capacity as you're likely to get.

A new era of cutthroat energy competition is upon us.

The agency's experts claim, however, that this will not prove quite the challenge it might seem, because they have also revised downward their projections of future energy *demand*. Back in 2005, they were projecting world oil consumption in 2025 at 119.2 million barrels per day, just below anticipated output at that time. This year—and we should all theoretically breathe a deep sigh of relief—the report projects that 2025 figure at only 101.1 million barrels per day, conveniently just what the world is expected to produce at that time. If this actually proves the case, then oil prices will presumably remain within a manageable range.

In fact, however, the consumption part of this equation seems like the less reliable calculation, especially if economic growth continues at anything like its recent pace in China and India. Indeed, all evidence suggests that growth in these countries will resume its pre-crisis pace by the end of 2009 or early 2010. Under those circumstances, global oil demand will eventually outpace supply, driving up prices again and threatening recurring and potentially disastrous economic disorders—possibly on the scale of the present global economic meltdown.

To have the slightest chance of averting such disasters means seeing a sharp rise in unconventional fuel output. Such fuels include Canadian oil sands, Venezuelan extra-heavy oil, deep-offshore oil, Arctic oil, shale oil, liquids derived from coal (coal-to-liquids or CTL), and biofuels. At present, these cumulatively constitute only about 4% of the world's liquid fuel supply but are expected to reach nearly 13% by 2030. All told, according to estimates in the new IEO report, unconventional liquid production will reach an estimated 13.4 million barrels per day in 2030, up from a projected 9.7 million barrels in the 2008 edition.

But for an expansion on this scale to occur, whole new industries will have to be created to manufacture such fuels at a cost of several trillion dollars. This undertaking, in turn, is provoking a wide-ranging debate over the environmental consequences of producing such fuels.

For example, any significant increase in biofuels use—assuming such fuels were produced by chemical means rather than, as now, by cooking—could substantially reduce emissions of carbon dioxide and other greenhouse gases, actually slowing the tempo of future climate change. On the other hand, any increase in the production of Canadian oil sands, Venezuelan extra-heavy oil, and Rocky Mountain shale oil will entail energy-intensive activities at staggering levels, sure to emit vast amounts of CO_2, which might more than cancel out any gains from the biofuels.

In addition, increased biofuels production risks the diversion of vast tracts of arable land from the crucial cultivation of basic food staples to the manufacture of transportation fuel. If, as is likely, oil prices continue to rise, expect it to be ever more attractive for farmers to grow more corn and other crops for eventual conversion to transportation fuels, which means rises in food costs that could price basics out of the range of the very poor, while stretching working families to the limit. As in May and June of 2008, when food riots spread across the planet in response to high food prices—caused, in part, by the diversion of vast amounts of corn acreage to biofuel production—this could well lead to mass unrest and mass starvation.

The usually optimistic analysts at the Department of Energy now believe global fuel supplies will simply not be able to keep pace with rising world energy demands.

A Heavy Energy Footprint on the Planet

The geopolitical implications of this transformation could well be striking. Among other developments, the global clout of Canada, Venezuela, and Brazil—all key producers of unconventional fuels—is bound to be strengthened.

Canada is becoming increasingly important as the world's leading producer of oil sands, or bitumen—a thick, gooey, viscous material that must be dug out of the ground and treated in various energy-intensive ways before it can be converted into synthetic petroleum fuel (synfuel). According to the IEO report, oil sands production, now at 1.3 million barrels a day and barely profitable, could hit the 4.4 million barrel mark (or even, according to the most optimistic scenarios, 6.5 million barrels) by 2030.

Given the IEA's new projections, this would represent an extraordinary addition to global energy supplies just when key sources of conventional oil in places like Mexico and the North Sea are expected to suffer severe declines. The extraction of oil sands, however, could prove a pollution disaster of the first order. For one thing, remarkable infusions of old-style energy are needed to extract this new energy, huge forest tracts would have to be cleared, and vast quantities of water used for the steam necessary to dislodge the buried goo (just as the equivalent of "peak water" may be arriving).

To have the slightest chance of averting such disasters means seeing a sharp rise in unconventional fuel output.

What this means is that the accelerated production of oil sands is sure to be linked to environmental despoliation, pollution, and global warming. There is considerable doubt that Canadian officials and the general public will, in the end, be willing to pay the economic and environmental price involved. In other words, whatever the IEA may project now, no one can know whether synfuels will really be available in the necessary quantities 15 or 20 years down the road.

Venezuela has long been an important source of crude oil for the United States, generating much of the revenue used by President Hugo Chávez to sustain his social experiments at home and an ambitious anti-American political agenda abroad. In the coming years, however, its production of conventional petroleum is expected to fall, leaving the country increasingly reliant on the exploitation of large deposits of bitumen in the eastern Orinoco River basin. Just to develop these "extra-heavy oil" deposits will require significant financial and energy investments and, as with Canadian oil sands, the environmental impact could be devastating. Nevertheless, successful development of these deposits could prove an economic bonanza for Venezuela.

The big winner in these grim energy sweepstakes, however, is likely to be Brazil. Already a major producer of ethanol, it is expected to see a huge increase in unconventional oil output once its new ultra-deep fields in the "subsalt" Campos and Santos basins come on line. These are massive offshore oil deposits buried beneath thick layers of salt some 100 miles off the coast of Rio de Janeiro and several miles beneath the ocean's surface.

When the substantial technical challenges to exploiting these undersea fields are overcome, Brazil's output could soar by as much as three million barrels per day. By 2030, Brazil should be a major player in the world energy equation, having succeeded Venezuela as South America's leading petroleum producer.

New Powers, New Problems

The IEO report hints at other geopolitical changes occurring in the global energy landscape, especially an expected stunning increase in the share of the global energy supply consumed in Asia and a corresponding decline by the United States, Japan, and other "First World" powers. In 1990, the developing nations of Asia and the Middle East accounted for only 17% of world energy consumption; by 2030, that number, the report suggests, should reach 41%, matching that of the major First World powers.

All recent editions of the report have predicted that China would eventually overtake the United States as number one energy consumer. What's notable is how quickly the 2009 edition expects that to happen. The 2006 report had China assuming the leadership position in a 2026–2030 time frame; in

2007, it was 2021–2024; in 2008, it was 2016–2020. This year, the EIA is projecting that China will overtake the United States between 2010 and 2014.

It's easy enough to overlook these shifting estimates, since the reports don't emphasize how they have changed from year to year. What they suggest, however, is that the United States will face ever fiercer competition from China in the global struggle to secure adequate supplies of energy to meet national needs.

Given what we have learned about the dwindling prospects for adequate future oil supplies, we are sure to face increased geopolitical competition and strife between the two countries in those few areas that are capable of producing additional quantities of oil (and undoubtedly genuine desperation among many other countries with far less resources and power).

And much else follows: As the world's leading energy consumer, Beijing [the capital of the People's Republic of China] will undoubtedly play a far more critical role in setting international energy policies and prices, undercutting the pivotal role long played by Washington[,D.C., the capital of the United States]. It is not hard to imagine, then, that major oil producers in the Middle East and Africa will see it as in their interest to deepen political and economic ties with China at the expense of the United States. China can also be expected to maintain close ties with oil providers like Iran and Sudan, no matter how this clashes with American foreign policy objectives.

At first glance, the *International Energy Outlook* for 2009 hardly looks different from previous editions: a tedious compendium of tables and text on global energy trends. Looked at another way, however, it trumpets the headlines of the future—and their news is not comforting.

The global energy equation is changing rapidly, and with it is likely to come great power competition, economic peril, rising starvation, growing unrest, environmental disaster, and shrinking energy supplies, no matter what steps are taken. No doubt the 2010 edition of the report and those that follow will reveal far more, but the new trends in energy on the planet are already increasingly evident—and unsettling.

Peak Oil Is a Myth

Jason Schwarz

Jason Schwarz works as chief options strategist for Lone Peak Asset Management and writes for financial Web sites such as The Street.com and Seeking Alpha as well as a number of national newspapers and magazines.

The data is becoming conclusive that peak oil is a myth. High oil prices are doing their job as oil exploration is flush with new finds:

1. An offshore find by Brazilian state oil company Petrobras in partnership with BG Group and Repsol-YPF may be the world's biggest discovery in 30 years, the head of the National Petroleum Agency said. A deepwater exploration area could contain as much as 33 billion barrels of oil, an amount that would nearly triple Brazil's reserves and make the offshore bloc the world's third-largest known oil reserve. "This would lay to rest some of the peak oil pronouncements that we were out of oil, that we weren't going to find any more and that we have to change our way of life," said Roger Read, an energy analyst and managing director at New York-based investment bank Natixis Bleichroeder Inc.

2. A trio of oil companies led by Chevron Corp. has tapped a petroleum pool deep beneath the Gulf of Mexico that could boost U.S. reserves by more than 50 percent. A test well indicates it could be the biggest new domestic oil discovery since Alaska's Prudhoe Bay a generation ago. Chevron estimated the 300-square-mile region where its test well sits could hold up to 15 billion barrels of oil and natural gas.

Jason Schwarz, "The 'Peak Oil' Myth: New Oil Is Plentiful," Seeking Alpha, June 22, 2008. http://seekingalpha.com. Reproduced by permission of the author.

3. Kosmos Energy says its oil field at West Cape Three Points is the largest discovery in deepwater West Africa and potentially the largest single field discovery in the region.

4. A new oil discovery has been made by Statoil [a Norwegian oil company] in the Ragnarrock prospect near the Sleipner area in the North Sea. "It is encouraging that Statoil has made an oil discovery in a little-explored exploration model that is close to our North Sea infrastructure," says Frode Fasteland, acting exploration manager for the North Sea.

5. Shell is currently analyzing and evaluating the well data of their own find in the Gulf of Mexico to determine the next steps. This find is rumored to be capable of producing 100 billion barrels. Operating in ultra-deep waters of the Gulf of Mexico, the Perdido spar will float on the surface in nearly 8,000 ft of water and is capable of producing as much as 130,000 barrels of oil equivalent per day.

6. In Iraq, excavators have struck three oil fields with reserves estimated at about 2 billion barrels, Kurdish region's Oil Minister Ashti Horami said.

7. Iran has discovered an oil field within its southwest Jofeir oil field that is expected to boost Jofeir's oil output to 33,000 barrels per day. Iran's new discovery is estimated to have reserves of 750 million barrels, according to Iran's Oil Minister, Gholam Hossein Nozari.

8. The United States holds significant oil shale resources underlying a total area of 16,000 square miles. This represents the largest known concentration of oil shale in the world and holds an estimated 1.5 trillion barrels of oil with 800 billion recoverable barrels—enough to meet U.S. demand for oil at current levels for 110 years. More than 70 percent of American oil shale is on federal land,

primarily in Colorado, Utah, and Wyoming. In Utah, a developer says his company already has the technology to produce 4,000 barrels a day using a furnace that can heat up rock using its own fuel. "This is not a science project," said Daniel G. Elcan, managing director of Oil Shale Exploration Corp. "For many years, the high cost of extracting oil from shale exceeded the benefit. But today the calculus is changing," President George Bush said. Sen. Orrin Hatch, R-Utah [Republican-Utah], said the country has to do everything it can to boost energy production. "We have as much oil in oil shale in Utah, Wyoming and Colorado as the rest of the world combined," he said.

9. In western North Dakota there is a formation known as the Bakken Shale. The formation extends into Montana and Canada. Geologists have estimated the area holds hundreds of billions of barrels of oil. In an interview provided by USGS [U.S. Geological Survey], scientist Brenda Pierce put the North Dakota oil in context. "Of the current USGS estimates, this is the largest oil accumulation in the lower 48," Pierce says. "It is also the largest continuous type of oil accumulation that we have ever assessed." The USGS study says with today's technology, about 4 billion barrels of oil can be pumped from the Bakken formation. By comparison, the 4 billion barrels in North Dakota represent less than half the oil in the Arctic National Wildlife Refuge, which has an estimated 10 billion barrels of recoverable oil.

Peak Oil Is a Scam

The peak oil theory is a moneymaking scam put out by the speculators looking for high commodity returns in a challenging market environment. Most of the above-mentioned finds have occurred in the last two years alone. I didn't even mention the untapped Alaskan oil fields or the recent Danish and

Australian finds. In the long term, crude prices will find stability at historic norms because there is no supply problem. How much longer will investors ignore these new oil finds? Probably until they can find other investment alternatives, which won't happen in the broad market until financials stop hemorrhaging. Respect the trend but understand that this is a bubble preparing to burst. When oil hit its high of $139 [per barrel, in June 2008; it later reached $147.27 per barrel on July 11, 2008] it represented more than a 600% increase in crude since the bull market began, returns eerily similar to the dot-com craze.

The peak oil theory is a moneymaking scam put out by the speculators looking for high commodity returns in a challenging market environment.

There are many theories that sound good but just aren't true. Take [former vice president] Al Gore's global warming crusade. It sounded great, it made perfect sense, but there was just one problem: The facts didn't support it. It seems that the masses who were loudly calling for a global warming crisis have shifted their energies to oil. We are bombarded on a daily basis by those who tell us that we should be fearful. They spin good news into bad. The latest absurdity had Goldman Sachs telling investors that China's 18% price increase will actually increase demand! That's a new one. Just like global warming, the rationale for peak oil sounds great, it makes sense, but there is just one small problem: The facts don't support it.

Oil Will Be a Growth Business for the Next Twenty Years

Daniel Yergin

Daniel Yergin is chairman of IHS Cambridge Energy Research Associates (IHS CERA), a leading global source of energy information, analysis, and software, and author of the book The Prize: The Epic Quest for Oil, Money & Power.

On Aug. 28, 1859, in the backwoods of northwest Pennsylvania, the first successful oil well went into production in the United States, ushering in an energy revolution that would make whale oil obsolete and eventually transform the industrial world. Yet 150 years later, even as demand increases in developing countries, oil's position in the global economy is being questioned and challenged as never before.

The Debate About Oil

Why this debate about the single most important source of energy—and a very convenient one—that provides 40% of the world's total energy? There are the traditional concerns—energy security, diversification, political risk, and the potential for conflict among nations over resources. The huge shifts in global income flows raise anxieties about the possible impact on the global balance of power. Some worry that physical supply will run out, although examination of the world's resource base—including a new analysis of over 800 oil fields—shows ample physical resources below ground. The politics above ground is a separate question.

But two new factors are now fueling the debate. One is the way in which oil has taken on a second identity. It is no longer only a physical commodity. It has also become a financial asset, along with stocks, bonds, currencies and the rest of the world's financial portfolio. The resulting price volatility—from less than $40 in 2004, to as high as $147.27 in July 2008, back down to $32.40 in December 2008, and now back over $70—has enormous consequences, and not only at the gas station and in terms of public anger. It makes it much more difficult to plan future energy investments, whether in oil and gas or in renewable and alternative fuels. And it can have enormous economic impact; Detroit [a major center of automobile manufacturing] was sent reeling by what happened at the gas pump in 2007 and 2008 even before the credit crisis. Such volatility can fuel future recessions and inflation.

Examination of the world's [oil] resource base . . . shows ample physical resources below ground. The politics above ground is a separate question.

That volatility has become an explosive political issue. British Prime Minister Gordon Brown and French President Nicolas Sarkozy recently called in these pages for a global solution to "destructive volatility," although they added that there are "no easy solutions."

The other new factor is climate change. Whatever the outcome of the upcoming mammoth United Nations climate-change conference in Copenhagen this December [2009], carbon regulation is now part of the future of oil.

Increasing Demand

But are big cuts in world oil usage possible? Both the U.S. Department of Energy and the International Energy Agency project that global energy use will increase almost 50% between 2006 and 2030—with oil still providing 30% or more of the world's energy.

The reason is something else that is new—the globalization of demand. No longer are the growth markets for petroleum to be found in North America, Western Europe and Japan. The United States has already hit "peak gasoline demand."

[Oil price volatility] makes it much more difficult to plan future energy investments, whether in oil and gas or in renewable and alternative fuels.

The demand growth has now shifted, massively, to the fast-growing emerging markets—China, India and the Middle East. Between 2000 and 2007, 85% of the growth in world oil demand was in the developing world. This shift continues: This year, more new cars have been sold in China than in the United States. When economic recovery takes hold, what happens in emerging countries will be the defining factor in the path for overall consumption.

There are two obvious ways to temper demand growth—either roll back economic growth, or find new technologies. The former is not acceptable. Thus, the answer has to lie in technology. The challenge is to find alternatives to oil that can be economically competitive—and convenient and reliable—at the massive scale required.

Alternatives to Oil?

What will those alternatives be? Batteries and plug-ins and other electric cars—today's favorite? Advanced biofuels? Natural-gas vehicles? The evolving smart grid, which can integrate plug-ins with greener electric generation? Or advances in the internal combustion engine, increasing fuel efficiency two or three times over?

In truth, we don't know, and we won't know for some time. For now, however, it is clear that the much higher levels of support for innovation—and large government incentives and subsidies—will inevitably drive technological change.

For oil, the focus is on transportation. After all, only 2% of America's electricity is generated by oil. Until recently, it appeared that the race between the electric car and the gasoline-powered car had been decided a century ago, with a decisive win by the gasoline-powered car on the basis of cost and performance. But the race is clearly on again.

Yet, whatever the breakthroughs, the actual impact on fuel use for the next 20 years will be incremental due to the time it takes to get large-scale mass production up and running and the massive scale of the global auto industry. My firm, IHS CERA, projects that with aggressive sales volumes and no major bumps in the road (unusual for new technologies), plug-in hybrids and pure electric vehicles could constitute 25% of new car sales by 2030. But because of the slow turnover of the overall fleet, gasoline consumption would be reduced only modestly below what it would otherwise be. Thereafter, of course, the impact could grow, perhaps very substantially.

But, in the U.S., at least for the next two decades, greater efficiency in the internal combustion engine, advanced diesels, and regular hybrids, combined with second-generation biofuels and new lighter materials, would have a bigger impact sooner. There is, however, a global twist. If small, low-cost electric vehicles really catch on in the auto growth markets in Asia, that would certainly lower the global growth curve for future oil demand.

As to the next 150 years of petroleum, we can hardly even begin to guess. For the next 20 years at least, the unfolding economic saga in emerging markets will continue to make oil a global growth business.

Humans Will Find a Better Energy Source Long Before Oil Runs Out

Brian Dunning

Brian Dunning is a computer scientist from Southern California and founder of Skeptoid: Critical Analysis of Pop Phenomena, *a weekly pro-science, anti-pseudoscience podcast and Web site.*

Think back to the days following 9/11 [2001 terrorist attacks], when all commercial and civilian air traffic was grounded. People were stranded everywhere. Only take it a step further: Take away the trains, the buses, and the rental cars. Imagine every gas station closed, and cars abandoned on the roadside as they too run out. People can't get to work and the nation's businesses can't even declare bankruptcy because there's no way to get to the courthouse to file the papers. The mail stops. Supermarkets are empty because there are no delivery trucks. And then, in a final shriek of terror, the power plants shut down, darkness falls everywhere, water pressure stops, and humanity devolves into a battlefield of hand-to-hand combat over who gets to eat the neighbor's dog.

This is the extremist scenario painted by peak oil advocates. Peak oil refers to the point at which world oil production must start to decline as reserves are emptied and pumps run dry. Oil is a finite resource, and so there's no doubt that at some point, peak oil will occur. The world's appetite for oil continues to grow exponentially, fueled by the explosive growth of most of the world's population in China and India. When the rift between increasing demand and decreasing supply gets to a breaking point, advocates say that the apocalyptic scenario described above must happen.

Pessimism and Optimism

In some places, peak oil has already happened. In the United States [US], oil production peaked about 1970, when we produced about 3.4 billion barrels per year. Today we produce about 1.5 billion. The curve has followed the 1956 prediction by American geophysicist M. King Hubbert who described the oil production of any given region over time as a bell curve. This is called Hubbert's curve. Every region in the world has its own separate curve. Some, like the US, are already on the downside. Others, like Canada, which is just beginning to exploit its oil sands, are only just now hitting the steepest climb on the upside. In addition to Canada, the Middle East and China are also still climbing their upsides. Russia has just barely tipped past its peak. The most pessimistic estimates for world peak oil say that it's already happened; the most optimistic give us another 30 years before we peak.

Oil is a finite resource, and so there's no doubt that at some point, peak oil will occur.

Oil production in any given region is not determined simply by physical factors such as the amount of reserves remaining and the technology required to develop it, but also by political and economic pressures. For example, Russia peaked way back in the Soviet days when their economy was falling apart, but their oil industry recovered throughout the 1990s and they've managed to find a second peak. The same could happen in the United States, if continental shelf and Rocky Mountain reserves were to be developed. They probably won't be, due to political pressures, but it's nice to know that they could be, if things came down to eating your neighbor's dog.

Human Adaptation Underestimated

The biggest error made by the peak oil doomsayers is in failing to recognize the adaptive nature of the world economy.

When demand goes up and supply goes down, prices go up, and consumers look to alternatives. As alternatives become more popular than the original, prices drop in reaction to the reduced demand, and eventually a marginalized industry disappears. Markets react and adapt. Currently [2008], we have very high gasoline prices. Consumers are reacting by clamoring for alternative fuel vehicles. Many industrial products depend on oil, such as fertilizers, solvents, and plastics to name only a few; and as the price of producing these climbs, industry turns to alternatives. Alternatives become increasingly commoditized and prices come down. Oil becomes less relevant, and eventually nobody will care when reserves finally do run dry.

The biggest error made by the peak oil doomsayers is in failing to recognize the adaptive nature of the world economy.

If consumers and industry failed to react to oil prices that climb astronomically for decades, then yes, it could be possible that we'd have an overnight shutdown of everything and the world would turn into a tumultuous battlefield of cannibalism. But neither consumers nor industry have ever acted this way, don't now, and aren't likely to in the future. Everyone wants to spend less money, and the most expensive options will always be least desirable.

Part of the reason that the doomsayers don't see this is that what's most visible right now is gasoline prices, and the total nonexistence of any viable alternative fuel vehicles. That's our worldview: expensive gas, diminishing production, no alternatives. But outside of this worldview, some very interesting things are happening. Believe it or not, tremendous research is going on to develop alternative fuel vehicles: supercapacitor technologies, fuel cells, hydrogen production. Silicon Valley is investing into alternative energy like a bat out of hell. And worldwide, industry is developing alternatives to petroleum-based plastic like fructose. Agricultural fertilizers can be made from seawater or atmospheric nitrogen, but they're not in production because the market has not yet reacted that far. Eventually, when the price gap closes, these non-oil-based sources may become the inexpensive standards.

Tremendous research is going on to develop alternative fuel vehicles: supercapacitor technologies, fuel cells, hydrogen production.

Other Resources

What about other resources? Do they peak as well? Yes, they do, at least nonrenewable ones do. It's generally believed that we're either just past or right about at the peak of gold production. Some 150,000 tons of gold have been mined throughout history, and the US Geological Survey estimates that there's another 90,000 tons still out there. Considering there's been a constant increase in gold mining efficiency, this all sounds about right. In many countries around the world, gold production has been dropping in recent years as reserves have been tapped out. But, do we need to expect a worldwide panic over gold? Probably not, since it's largely a luxury item and its industrial uses are relatively modest. We expect to see prices rise as supply diminishes, and probably a number of market adjustments until we settle into an eventual equilibrium of old gold being reused to meet demand.

There are other more serious resource peaks. Peak phosphorous, for one. Phosphorous is a crucial ingredient of both synthetic and organic crop fertilizers. And glyophosphate is a principal ingredient in herbicides used in super-high-yield genetically modified food crops. Both have seen dramatic price hikes in recent years as rock phosphate, the source of nearly all industrial phosphorus, is being mined out. If I stopped talking now, this would seem an alarming, terrifying prospect, and you might see doom & gloom Web sites predicting global disaster the way you do with peak oil. Peak phosphorus is a painful situation for farmers, but it's one that's not insoluble. In the short term, farmers invest in the phosphorus companies, thus offsetting their production costs with dividend income. In the long term, the fertilizer producers continue their research into alternative supplies. High on their list is seawater, which is after all, the eventual depository of all agricultural runoff. This proposal is essentially an accelerated leveraging of nature's existing cycle.

Another peak that we're starting to hear about is peak silicon. In this case, it's not a physical shortage of silicon; it's the engineering limits of what you can do with silicon to make computer chips. Such a peak would mean that the capabilities of computers could no longer grow with our increasing demand on them. The doomsayer pundits could make an argument here too that overnight we'll start eating each other and burning down our cities and running around with babies on pitchforks. But in fact what happens is that the silicon industry fades and the graphene industry rises. Graphene is only one of numerous next-generation computer chip technologies that obsolesce silicon.

What tends to happen in any industry, is that by the time an existing resource runs out, inventive scientists have already come up with something better.

Trusting the Future

Generally, what tends to happen in any industry, is that by the time an existing resource runs out, inventive scientists have already come up with something better. When a production peak looms (be it oil, phosphorus, silicon, or anything), this provides a kick in the pants to accelerate development. Market economies work in such a way that investors are encouraged to fund such development, and the bigger the looming problem, the bigger the investment to meet it.

Mark Twain used to speak nostalgically of the sad disappearance of the riverboat industry. It was killed by steam trains. Steam trains were later killed in turn by diesel electrics. The glory days of rail travel were ended by the advent of airlines. Eventually airliners aren't going to be able to burn jet fuel anymore. What will happen then? Today, I have no idea; much like Mark Twain had no idea that airliners would one day replace his beloved steamboat. To assume that the current state of technology represents the last and final stage of development is a completely ignorant viewpoint. To listen to the doomsayers is to be completely uncritical and un-skeptical. I don't know what's around tomorrow's corner, but all the evidence of history tells us that it's probably not a big scary dragon.

CHAPTER 4

How Does Oil Affect the Future?

Chapter Preface

Energy experts agree that the current world economy is dependent on oil and other fossil fuels. A growing consensus suggests that this dependence is increasingly dangerous, however, not only because of harm to the environment, but also because demand for energy is increasing in the developing world. If the oil supply is disrupted, if prices rise too high, or if supply cannot keep up with this demand, the world could see more intense competition for oil and other resources among nations—possibly even military confrontations. For all these reasons, a growing recognition exists in the United States and other countries that it will be necessary to discover and shift to alternative, environmentally friendly energy sources in the future to ensure global security.

Some say the most exciting possibilities for alternatives to oil are renewable energy sources that do not pollute the environment. Solar energy is one of the most attractive renewable options because the sun's energy is free and relatively easy to capture using solar panels. Today's solar panels use one of two methods. The first is thermal solar power, in which liquid (water or nontoxic antifreeze) circulates through tubing exposed to the sun and collects the heat. This method is good for on-site uses, such as residential hot water or in-floor home heating. The second method is photovoltaic power cells, often made of silicon, which produce electricity when the heat from the sun excites electrons in the silicon material. The electricity is then converted into AC 120-volt power, which is the type of electricity commonly used in homes and businesses, so the power can then be used to run any electrical appliance or system. It can also be used to charge batteries or be fed into the regular electrical power grid.

Silicon photovoltaic panels are relatively efficient, but the silicon used in these solar collectors is expensive, so there is an ongoing effort to research other technologies. The most promising of these is the thin-film solar cell, which is many times smaller in size than bulky solar panels. The newest materials used to make thin-film solar cells are cadmium telluride and copper indium gallium diselenide (CIGS)—materials that are much less expensive than silicon. Solar companies are working to make thin-film technology comparable to solar panels in efficiency and cost-effective enough to compete with fossil fuels. The hope is that solar technology will eventually allow cheap solar cells to be stamped onto a variety of products, such as roofing materials, parking lot covers, or even cars.

Wind power is also a growing type of renewable energy. Like solar power, it is free and easily harnessed. Although wind is dependent on weather conditions, some locations have very steady winds and are ideal for this type of power generation. This technology works by capturing the power of the wind using wind turbines, which produce electricity as they turn. The idea is similar to windmills used in earlier times, but much more sophisticated. In fact, some power companies have erected wind farms, where large numbers of immense turbines are constructed to produce electricity on a large scale and the power is then funneled into the electrical grid. Some people oppose the use of wind turbines because of aesthetics or the danger to birds, but most people do not seem to mind the visual impact of turbines and bird deaths are often considered fairly minor when compared to the widespread environmental effects of fossil fuel energies.

A third type of renewable energy that is attracting widespread interest is geothermal energy, which taps into heat stored in the earth's inner core. This heat is produced by hot and molten rock called magma that lies underneath the planet's surface crust, mostly from the decay of naturally radioactive materials such as uranium and potassium. Unlike solar and wind energy, therefore, geothermal power can be found almost anywhere, although temperatures are highest in locations near active or geologically young volcanoes. Energy is obtained from geothermal sources by tapping into naturally occurring hot springs that have already been heated by the magma; steam from the hot water can easily be captured and used to produce electricity. Geothermal plants typically use one of three different designs: (1) by sending steam directly to a turbine; (2) by depressurizing very hot water into steam, which is then used to turn a turbine; or (3) by sending the hot water through a heat exchanger, where it heats another liquid that can be more easily turned into steam to run the turbine. Geothermal power is also very useful for home heating and cooling—using a system that runs liquid through pipes placed underground, bringing up heat during cold weather and cold during hot weather, to keep temperatures in the home temperate.

Several other types of renewable energy technologies also may help provide clean energy in the future. One of these is tidal and wave power—a way of harnessing the movement of water in the oceans. Tidal power works by using the water that flows in and out with the tide to turn turbines to produce electricity. Wave power converts waves into electricity by placing devices in the ocean to use the movement to create electricity. Although they are not yet widely used, both of these technologies hold great potential for the future, especially in coastal areas with strong tide action.

An equally exciting type of energy technology is called biomass energy. Biomass refers to any kind of organic biological material, such as animal wastes, plant matter, crop or forest residue, or waste vegetable oils. These materials can be burned to create electricity directly or they can be converted into another chemical form through some form of heat—such as simple combustion, torrefaction (using high temperatures between 200 and 320 degrees Celsius), pyrolyisis (using temperatures above 300 degrees Celsius), or gasification (a process that mixes the organic material at very high temperatures with oxygen or steam to create a synthetic gas). The resulting end products—typically either a liquid or a gas—can then be used as fuel to heat homes or power vehicles. One type of biofuel is ethanol, which is already being used with or as an alternative to gasoline as an automotive fuel. Some energy experts advocate building flex-fuel vehicles that can run on either gasoline or ethanol.

Researchers are also working hard on developing another transportation fuel—hydrogen fuel cells. Hydrogen fuel cells are battery-like devices that can power vehicles using hydrogen and oxygen. The fuel cell basically converts these two materials into water, in the process producing electricity. As long as there is a supply of hydrogen, the fuel cells would continue to operate, unlike a battery, which goes dead after a certain period of time. Many companies are involved in this research, but some critics believe there are too many problems to overcome with this technology. For example, fuel cells are costly to produce and would require an infrastructure of hydrogen stations similar to today's gas stations to deliver the hydrogen fuel to consumers.

Which of these energy sources will take the place of oil in the future is not yet known, because the transition away from oil has just begun. Authors of the viewpoints in this chapter discuss the future of oil production and some of the obstacles that may lie ahead.

Oil Will Continue to Impact the Global Economy

Michael T. Klare

Michael T. Klare is Five College Professor of Peace and World Security Studies at Hampshire College in Amherst, Massachusetts, and author of the book Rising Powers, Shrinking Planet: The New Geopolitics of Energy.

Here ... is a simple but crucial reality to keep in mind: No matter how much it costs, whether it's rising or falling, oil has a profound impact on the world we inhabit. ...

The main reason? In good times and bad, oil will continue to supply the largest share of the world's energy supply. For all the talk of alternatives, petroleum will remain the number one source of energy for at least the next several decades. According to December 2008 projections from the U.S. Department of Energy (DOE), petroleum products will still make up 38% of America's total energy supply in 2015; natural gas and coal only 23% each. Oil's overall share is expected to decline slightly as biofuels (and other alternatives) take on a larger percentage of the total, but even in 2030—the furthest the DOE is currently willing to project—it will still remain the dominant fuel.

A similar pattern holds for the planet as a whole: Although biofuels and other renewable sources of energy are expected to play a growing role in the global energy equation, don't expect oil to be anything but the world's leading source of fuel for decades to come.

Oil's Influence

Keep your eye on the politics of oil and you'll always know a lot about what's actually happening on this planet. Low prices, as at present, are bad for producers, and so will hurt a number of countries that the U.S. government considers hostile, including Venezuela, Iran, and even that natural-gas-and-oil giant Russia. All of them have, in recent years, used their soaring oil income to finance political endeavors considered inimical to U.S. interests. However, dwindling prices could also shake the very foundations of oil allies like Mexico, Nigeria, and Saudi Arabia, which could experience internal unrest as oil revenues, and so state expenditures, decline.

In good times and bad, oil will continue to supply the largest share of the world's energy supply.

No less important, diminished oil prices discourage investment in complex oil ventures like deep-offshore drilling, as well as investment in the development of alternatives to oil like advanced (nonfood) biofuels. Perhaps most disastrously, in a cheap oil moment, investment in nonpolluting, non-climate-altering alternatives like solar, wind, and tidal energy is also likely to dwindle. In the longer term, what this means is that, once a global economic recovery begins, we can expect a fresh oil price shock as future energy options prove painfully limited.

Clearly, there is no escaping oil's influence. Yet it's hard to know just what forms this influence will take in the year. Nevertheless, here are three provisional observations on oil's fate— and so ours—in the year ahead.

1. The Price of Oil Will Remain Low Until It Begins to Rise Again: I know, I know: This sounds totally inane. It's just that there's no other way to put it. The price of oil has essentially dropped through the floor because, in the past four months, demand collapsed due to the onset of a staggering global recession. It is not likely to approach the record levels of spring and summer 2008 again until demand picks up and/or the global oil supply is curbed dramatically. At this point, unfortunately, no crystal ball can predict just when either of those events will occur.

The contraction in international demand has indeed been stunning. After rising for much of last summer [2008], demand plunged in the early fall by several hundred thousand barrels per day, producing a net decline for 2008 of 50,000 barrels per day. This year, the Department of Energy projects global demand to fall by a far more impressive 450,000 barrels per day—"the first time in three decades that world consumption would decline in two consecutive years."

Diminished oil prices discourage investment in complex oil ventures like deep-offshore drilling, as well as investment in the development of alternatives to oil.

Needless to say, these declines were unexpected. Believing that international demand would continue to grow—as had been the case in almost every year since the last big recession of 1980—the global oil industry steadily added to production capacity and was gearing up for more of the same in 2009 and beyond. Indeed, under intense pressure from the [George W.] Bush administration, the Saudis had indicated last June [2008] that they would gradually add to their capacity until they reached an extra 2.5 million barrels per day.

Today, the industry is burdened with excess output and insufficient demand—a surefire recipe for plunging oil prices. Even the December 17 [2008] decision by members of the Organization of [the] Petroleum Exporting Countries (OPEC) to reduce their collective output by 2.2 million barrels per day has failed to lead to a significant increase in prices. (Saudi Arabia's King Abdullah said recently that he considers $75 a barrel a "fair price" for oil.)

How long will the imbalance between demand and supply last? Until the middle of 2009, if not the end of the year, most analysts believe. Others suspect that a true global recovery will not even get under way until 2010, or later. It all depends on how deep and prolonged you expect the recession—or any coming depression—to be.

Today, the industry is burdened with excess output and insufficient demand—a surefire recipe for plunging oil prices.

A critical factor will be China's ability to absorb oil. After all, between 2002 and 2007, that country accounted for 35% of the total increase in world oil consumption—and, according to the DOE, it is expected to claim at least another 24% of any global increase in the coming decade. The upsurge in Chinese consumption, combined with unremitting demand from older industrialized nations and significant price speculation on oil futures, largely explained the astronomical way prices were driven up until last summer. But with the Chinese economy visibly faltering, such projections no longer seem valid. Many analysts now predict that a sharp drop-off in Chinese demand will only accelerate the downward journey of global energy prices. Under these conditions, an early price turnaround appears increasingly unlikely.

2. When Prices Do Rise Again, They Will Rise Sharply: At present, the world enjoys the (relatively) unfamiliar prospect of a global oil-production surplus, but there's a problematic aspect to this. As long as prices remain low, oil companies have no incentive to invest in costly new production ventures, which means no new capacity is being added to global inventories, while available capacity continues to be drained. Simply put, what this means is that, when demand begins to surge again, global output is likely to prove inadequate. As Ed Crooks of the *Financial Times* has suggested, "The plunging oil price is like a dangerously addictive painkiller: Short-term relief is being provided at a cost of serious long-term harm."

Signs of a slowdown in oil-output investment are already multiplying fast. Saudi Arabia, for example, has announced delays in four major energy projects in what appears to be a broad retreat from its promise to increase future output. Among the projects being delayed are a $1.2 billion venture to restart the historic Dammam oil field, development of the 900,000-barrel-per-day Manifa oil field, and construction of new refineries at Yanbu and Jubail. In each case, the delays are being attributed to reduced international demand. "We are going back to our partners and discussing with them the new economic circumstances," explained Kahled al-Buraik, an official of Saudi Aramco.

When demand begins to surge again, global output is likely to prove inadequate.

In addition, most "easy oil" reservoirs have now been exhausted, which means that virtually all remaining global reserves are going to be of the "tough oil" variety. These require extraction technology far too costly to be profitable at a moment when the per-barrel price remains under $50. Principal among these are exploitation of the tar sands of Canada and of deep offshore fields in the Gulf of Mexico, the Gulf of Guinea, and waters off Brazil. While such potential reserves undoubtedly harbor significant supplies of petroleum, they won't return a profit until the price of oil reaches $80 or more per barrel—nearly twice what it is fetching today. Under these circumstances, it is hardly surprising that the oil majors are cancelling or postponing plans for new projects in Canada and these offshore locations.

"Low oil prices are very dangerous for the world economy," commented Mohamed bin Dhaen Al Hamli, the United Arab Emirates' energy minister, at a London oil-industry conference in October. With prices dropping, he noted, "a lot of projects that are in the pipeline are going to be reassessed."

With industry cutting back on investment, there will be less capacity to meet rising demand when the world economy does rebound. At that time, expect the present situation to change with predictably startling rapidity, as rising demand suddenly finds itself chasing inadequate supply in an energy-deficit world.

When this will occur and how high oil prices will then climb cannot, of course, be known, but expect gas-pump shock. It's possible that the energy shock to come will be no less fierce than the present global recession and energy price collapse. The Department of Energy, in its most recent projections, predicts that oil will reach an average of $78 per barrel in 2010, $110 in 2015, and $116 in 2020. Other analysts suggest that prices could go much higher much faster, especially if demand picks up quickly and the oil companies are slow to restart projects now being put on hold.

3. Low Oil Prices, Like High Ones, Will Have Significant Worldwide Political Implications: The steady run-up in oil prices between 2003 and 2008 was the result of a sharp increase in global demand as well as a perception that the international energy industry was having difficulty bringing sufficient new sources of supply online. Many analysts spoke of the imminent arrival of "peak oil," the moment at which global output would commence an irreversible decline. All this fueled fierce efforts by major consuming nations to secure control over as many foreign sources of petroleum as they could, including frenzied attempts by U.S., European, and Chinese firms to gobble up oil concessions in Africa and the Caspian Sea basin—the theme of my latest book, *Rising Powers, Shrinking Planet: The New Geopolitics of Energy*.

With the plunge in oil prices and a growing sense (however temporary) of oil plenty, this dog-eat-dog competition is likely to abate. The current absence of intense competition does not, however, mean that oil prices will cease to have an impact on global politics. Far from it. In fact, *low* prices are just as likely to roil the international landscape, only in new ways. While competition among consuming states may lessen, negative political conditions within producing nations are sure to be magnified.

Many of these nations, including Angola, Iran, Iraq, Mexico, Nigeria, Russia, Saudi Arabia, and Venezuela, among others, rely on income from oil exports for a large part of their government expenditures, using this money to finance health and education, infrastructure improvements, food and energy subsidies, and social welfare programs. Soaring energy prices, for instance, allowed many producer countries to reduce high youth unemployment—and so potential unrest. As prices come crashing down, governments are already being forced to cut back on programs that aid the poor, the middle class, and the unemployed, which is already producing waves of instability in many parts of the world.

Russia's state budget, for example, remains balanced only when oil prices stay at or above $70 per barrel. With government income dwindling, the Kremlin has been forced to dig into accumulated reserves in order to meet its obligations and prop up sinking companies as well as the sinking ruble. The nation hailed as an energy giant is running out of money quickly. Unemployment is on the rise, and many firms are reducing work hours to save cash. Although Prime Minister Vladimir Putin remains popular, the first signs of public discontent have begun to appear, including scattered protests against increased tariffs on imported goods, rising public transit fees, and other such measures.

The decline in oil prices has been particularly damaging to natural gas behemoth Gazprom, Russia's biggest company and the source (in good times) of approximately one quarter of government tax income. Because the price of natural gas is usually pegged to that of oil, declining oil prices have hit the company hard: Last summer, CEO Alexey Miller estimated its market value at $360 billion; today, it's $85 billion.

In the past, the Russians have used gas shutoffs to neighboring states to extend their political clout. Given the steep drop in gas prices, however, Gazprom's January 1st [2009] decision to sever gas supplies to Ukraine (for failure to pay for $1.5 billion in past deliveries) is, at least in part, finance-based. Though the decision has triggered energy shortages in Europe—25% of its natural gas arrives via Gazprom-fueled pipelines that traverse Ukraine—Moscow shows no sign of backing down in the price dispute. "They do need the money," observed Chris Weafer of UralSib Bank in Moscow. "That is the bottom line."

Plunging oil prices are also expected to place severe strains on the governments of Iran, Saudi Arabia, and Venezuela, all of which benefited from the record prices of the past few years to finance public works, subsidize basic necessities, and generate employment. Like Russia, these countries adopted expansive budgets on the assumption that a world of $70 or more per barrel gas prices would continue indefinitely. Now, like other affected producers, they must dip into accumulated reserves, borrow at a premium, and cut back on social spending—all of which risk a rise in political opposition and unrest at home.

Prices will eventually rise again, perhaps some year soon, swiftly and to new record heights.

The government of Iran, for example, has announced plans to eliminate subsidies on energy (gasoline now costs 36 cents per gallon)—a move expected to spark widespread protests in a country where unemployment rates and living costs are rising precipitously. The Saudi government has promised to avoid budget cuts for the time being by drawing on accumulated reserves, but unemployment is growing there as well.

Diminished spending in oil-producing states like Kuwait, Saudi Arabia, and the United Arab Emirates will also affect nonproducing countries like Egypt, Jordan, and Yemen because young men from these countries migrate to the oil kingdoms when times are flush in search of higher-paying jobs. When times are rough, however, they are the first to be laid off and are often sent back to their homelands where few jobs await them.

All this is occurring against the backdrop of an upsurge in the popularity of Islam, including its more militant forms that reject the "collaborationist" politics of pro-U.S. regimes like those of Hosni Mubarak of Egypt and King Abdullah II of Jordan. Combine this with the recent devastating Israeli air attacks on, and ground invasion of, Gaza as well as the seemingly lukewarm response of moderate Arab regimes to the plight of the 1.5 million Palestinians trapped in that tiny strip of land, and the stage may be set for a major upsurge in anti-government unrest and violence. If so, no one will see this as oil-related, and yet that, in part, is what it will be.

In the context of a planet caught in the grip of a fierce economic downturn, other stormy energy scenarios involving key oil-producing countries are easy enough to imagine. When and where they will arise cannot be foreseen, but such eruptions are only likely to make any future era of rising energy prices all that much more difficult. And, indeed, prices will eventually rise again, perhaps some year soon, swiftly and to new record heights. At that point, we will be confronted with the sort of problems we faced in the spring and summer of 2008, when raging demand and inadequate supply drove petroleum costs ever skyward. In the meantime, it's important to remember that, even with prices as low as they are, we cannot escape the consequences of our addiction to oil.

Rising Oil Prices May Threaten Oil Production and Supply

Greenpeace

Greenpeace is an international environmental organization that works to directly confront people and governments that harm the environment.

This second update to our *Rising Risks* report builds on earlier work examining the structural macroeconomic threats to tar sands production. . . . The resulting analysis is unsettling for the tar sands industry. It suggests that the international oil companies (IOCs) face significant challenges to their current business plans for oil production. While risk is nothing new to the oil industry, the kind of structural change being signalled today is unprecedented. Significantly, the implications are particularly salient not only for tar sands projects but also for other 'frontier' oil projects championed by the IOCs. Ultra-deepwater and offshore arctic resources face a similar challenge as, like tar sands oil, they also represent the 'marginal barrel'.

The main factors constituting this threat to the IOCs are:

- As former Shell CEO Jeroen van der Veer has said several times recently, the era of 'easy oil' is over. Persistent resource nationalism and depletion of conventional resources in Europe and North America has left the IOCs with difficult-to-access oil to divide between them. This means that the bulk of the oil that is left for them to exploit is to be found in the tar sands and in ultra-deepwater and other marginal resources such as the Arctic. This is reflected in the breakdown of their total resources, a longer term analysis of their reserves than those they disclose as 'proven' or 'probable'.

- All of these resources are very expensive to produce, require long lead-in times to bring onstream and in many cases have controversial environmental and social impacts that will cost more to ameliorate. The expense of bringing much of this oil to market means that the sustained oil price needed to do so is dangerously close to a 'break point' price beyond which oil demand is constrained via changes in consumer behavior and re-duced economic growth.

- While the oil price may at times rise above that ceiling, the consequence is demand destruction and price dete-rioration. We are still in the midst of a particularly ag-gressive cycle of this phenomenon.

- The difference between the recovery periods following previous oil shocks and the current one is that a sig-nificant proportion of today's oil demand decline is permanent. In other words, this recession has triggered demand destruction as well as demand suppression.

- This demand destruction is driven by the disintegration of market barriers to significant improvements in effi-ciency, and transportation technology diversity, which are in turn driven by both consumer sentiment and government policy aimed at addressing energy security, limiting exposure to oil price volatility and addressing climate change.

- As a result, oil demand in the US [United States] and OECD [Organisation for Economic Co-operation and Development, an international group with 30 member countries] has peaked.

- While demand in non-OECD countries still has significant growth potential, it is unlikely to grow at the rates that were being predicted before the recession, and may also peak within the coming decade. Therefore a global peak in oil demand may be within sight. The implications of this for the high cost production that IOCs increasingly face are extremely serious.

- The issue of the steep decline in traditional oil supplies that some refer to as 'peak oil' may at times create 'supply squeezes' when supply declines at a greater rate than demand and prices will spike. But each supply squeeze will create further permanent demand destruction. When a demand peak is reached, the most expensive-to-extract oil will face a serious threat as OPEC [Organization for the Petroleum Exporting Countries] producers move to monetise their reserves in a significantly different market paradigm.

The era of 'easy oil' is over.

Oil Price Break Points

In December 2008, we commissioned Marc Brammer of Innovest (now RiskMetrics) to analyse the implications for the tar sands industry of an idea first proposed by Cambridge Energy Research Associates (CERA) in 2006. CERA discussed a 'break point' price for oil of between $100 and $120 per barrel. When oil rises above this price range, not only do alternative technologies become significantly more competitive but economic growth is constrained and thus oil consumption curtailed. This scenario played out dramatically in 2008 as in the first quarter of that year . . . the US economy went into recession as oil approached $100 a barrel.

Marc Brammer posited that the break-even point for new tar sands projects was close to the ceiling at which oil prices could be sustained by the economy. At between $65 and $90, the oft-quoted range for breakeven, the room for long-term profitability appears slender. He also pointed out that those break-even levels do not currently include costs that such projects are likely to see added in the near future:

> Should additional costs be considered such as the inevitable remediation costs, carbon costs and the potential inflationary costs for materials and labour that would be imposed by the very oil prices required for profitability, it does not appear that these projects are economically viable.

This theory has been vividly illustrated by events of the past year. The oil price rally above $100 lasted barely nine months. It was followed by a severe recession during which prices fell dramatically and most planned tar sands projects were deferred. With the global economy in a fragile state and oil prices rallying amid rumours of 'green shoots' in June 2009, discussion increasingly focused on whether the economy can withstand further price increases. UK [United Kingdom] Prime Minister Gordon Brown asked Treasury and Department of Business ministers to draft plans to cope with rising oil prices in June following an oil price rally that took prices beyond $70 a barrel.

A report from energy business analysts Douglas-Westwood gave a much more detailed analysis of the effect on the US economy of high oil prices, and set a lower threshold than CERA for the 'break point' effect. The report suggested that since the oil shock of 1973, 'when oil consumption breached 4% of GDP [gross domestic product], the US has suffered a recession, and indeed, the current US recession began within two months of oil hitting the 4% threshold, that is, when oil reached $80/bl [per barrel]'. The paper posited $80 per barrel as the 'recession threshold'.

But while there is an obvious concern about the negative effect on economic growth of high oil prices, it would appear that there is another factor for oil producers to be concerned about. At the launch of BP's [British Petroleum's] *Statistical Review of World Energy* in early June 2009, BP's chief executive Tony Hayward said that as the oil price went over $90 consumers 'began to change their behaviour' and that there was significant 'elasticity of demand above $100 a barrel'. He suggested that the 'right range' for the oil price would be between $60–90 a barrel, as below that level suppliers 'shut in investment and stop doing activity'.

If Hayward and Douglas-Westwood are accurate in their assessment, it would appear that oil demand is curtailed by constrained economic growth and consumer behaviour at oil prices between $80–90/bl. That leaves tar sands producers even less of a margin than that suggested by CERA in 2006. But surely as economic growth picks up so will demand, and supply constraints caused by depletion and underinvestment will ensure high oil prices in the future? Won't people just have to pay the price for oil? It would appear that there are a number of shifts on the horizon that seriously challenge that thinking.

A little earlier in the Q&A [question and answer] session following the presentation of BP's 2009 *Statistical Review of World Energy*, Tony Hayward was asked whether the volatility seen in the oil market in 2008 was a signal of the much-anticipated peak in global oil supply. His answer was probably not what the questioner was expecting to hear:

> BP is unlikely to sell more gasoline ever in the United States [. . .] than it sold in the first half of 2008. The energy efficiency drive that is going to come through over the next few years will mean that demand in the mature markets of the OECD will continue to decline. I think the real question is what is the projection of future demand? . . .

China's Role in Increasing Demand

With OECD demand in decline, China's share of global primary energy growth in 2008 grew to 75%, while its oil demand grew 3.3% in the face of a global decline of 0.6%. It is clear that China now plays a pivotal role in the global oil demand trajectory. In short, its demand growth could outweigh declines elsewhere, whereas a more restrained rate of post-recession demand growth could signal a demand peak.

A global peak in oil demand may be within sight. The implications of this . . . are extremely serious.

A major indicator of China's concern over its oil demand came in May 2009 when government officials drafted new standards to achieve significant improvement in vehicle fuel efficiency by 2015. Commentators cited the multifaceted nature of China's interests in achieving this, which included energy security, urban pollution and climate change as well as the desire to increase China's competitiveness in the vehicle export market.

This is impressive, as new vehicles in China are already achieving an efficiency level roughly equivalent to the level the US has recently mandated for 2016 under new tighter CAFE [Corporate Average Fuel Economy] standards. This is approximately 56% higher than today's US standard. Under the proposed changes, cars sold in China will be 18% more efficient than this by 2015 by achieving 42.2 miles per gallon on average.

Another indicator of the Chinese government's willingness to act on fuel consumption came in June 2009, when the government unexpectedly raised pump prices to the highest level ever. Chinese consumers are paying approximately 12.5% more than their American counterparts following the 9 and 10% respective rise in petrol and diesel prices, the third rise since March this year.

These latest measures follow sales tax changes implemented last year that clearly demonstrate the government's thinking. Fuel-efficient family cars with engine sizes of 1.6 litres and under now pay sales tax at 1%, compared with up to 40% for bigger cars including minivans and sport-utility vehicles. The government's desire to support fuel-efficient vehicle manufacturing in China has been widely noted by international companies. Following the Shanghai Auto Show in April 2009, where nearly 1,000 cars featuring fuel-efficient technology were displayed, Ford's vice president for Asia, John Parker, told the *New York Times* that the company was preparing to transfer its efficiency technology to its Chinese joint venture and that he believed that the Chinese government's emphasis on efficiency was 'for keeps'.

[China's] demand growth could outweigh declines elsewhere.

GM's [General Motors'] regional executive Nick Reilly also told the paper that China was poised to be the leader in alternative-fuel vehicles.

> There's no question that the government and the companies here are spending huge amounts in this area, so there's no doubt they are going to be important players, [. . .] if you look at where batteries are making the fastest progress, it's China, it's Korea, it's where the government is heavily behind it.

He went on to comment on China's incentives:

> I think there's a very good chance China will lead [in alternative energy vehicles], because they've got the need, they've got the size of market, they've got the resources.

These trends in car manufacture have significant implications for the global market given that China overtook the US as the biggest car manufacturer globally in the first quarter of this year.

So while huge growth in car ownership is expected in China, each car is significantly less thirsty than its US counterpart, and will continue to improve in efficiency. Additionally, Chinese consumers are no longer protected from oil prices by national subsidies. Meanwhile there is strong evidence to suggest that the government sees tremendous opportunities for the country to lead the market in producing increasingly efficient vehicles. So what if a global peak in demand was to occur, perhaps around 2020 or maybe a little later? Where would that leave Shell, BP and the other IOCs? Have they the right strategies in place to cope with such a structural shift? What will be the impact on tar sands projects? Many of the tar sands investments they are currently considering whether to proceed with are now unlikely to come onstream before 2020, and they will require years to pay back capital and produce returns. . . .

Oil Companies' Concerns

So with an increasing proportion of IOC reserves concentrated in oil fields that will need upwards of $60 a barrel to make a profit, and evidence that high oil prices can only be sustained for short periods due to the impact on demand, are oil company executives showing concern about these risks? According to at least one survey, they are beginning to.

In April 2009 Ernst & Young produced its annual analysis of business risk in the oil and gas sector. The report's assessment was drawn from interviews with senior executives and analysts in the sector as well as the company's own experts. It showed that individuals in the sector were starting to express awareness of the threats we have highlighted here. Price volatility entered the list of the top ten risks faced by the sector. It was the first time the issue had made it onto the list, and it came in ranked at number three. Topping the list were long-term contenders: access to reserves and uncertain energy policy. . . .

It would appear that there are already concerns among senior analysts and executives in the oil and gas sector that

IOCs are not only vulnerable in their dependence on high-cost resources, but in the course of pursuing these risky projects they may be missing the opportunity to benefit from the real prize of the future energy market: the development of alternatives to oil.

Higher Oil Prices Could Strain Global Agriculture Systems

Jason Mark

Jason Mark lives and works on an organic farm in California. He is the coauthor, with Kevin Danaher, of the book Insurrection: Citizen Challenges to Corporate Power.

Farmer Richard Randall doesn't believe in the notion of "peak oil," the argument that civilization will soon experience an acute—and irreversible—petroleum scarcity that will fundamentally alter our way of life. A 61-year-old wheat and sorghum grower from Scott City, Kan., Randall says he's seen high oil prices before, and that today's expensive petroleum is just part of a natural market cycle that will eventually adjust itself, leading to lowered fuel costs.

"I think there's plenty of oil there," Randall said recently. "I feel that if we allow the marketplace to work without interruption in the supply, we will find a level. It's not going to be as low as it was, but it will come down. We do need to produce oil where we can."

Randall may not be certain when oil prices will level out, but it's abundantly clear to him that $70/barrel petroleum is taking a huge bite out of his business. Nearly every part of his farming operation is being impacted. The price for the diesel fuel that runs the tractors and tracks on his 4,500-acre farm [has] more than tripled in the last four years, rising from 80 cents per gallon to close to $3. Fertilizer prices are also up sharply. Since synthetic fertilizers are made from natural gas, they too are impacted by higher fossil fuel prices; the cost of fertilizer has gone from about $160 per ton to $460 per ton in the last three years. Smaller, organic growers are also feeling a pinch from costlier petroleum. The price for the plastic drip irrigation tape commonly used on organic fruit and vegetable farms is up 20 percent from two years ago.

Because farmers operate in a commodity market where buyers and brokers dictate the price of the harvest, high oil costs have been particularly painful. Unlike other businesses, farms have no way to pass their rising costs on to consumers.

Because farmers operate in a commodity market where buyers and brokers dictate the price of the harvest, high oil costs have been particularly painful.

"All of our expenses have gone up pretty well, but we can't put on a surcharge for fuel like everyone else can," Randall said. "It's made it a lot tougher."

Tomorrow's Crises

For farmers like Randall, today's challenges may be tomorrow's crises. The problems of coping with high oil prices reveal how utterly dependent our food production system is on nonrenewable fuels. As long as oil is plentiful, that dependence isn't a concern. But in some circles, fears are growing that if global petroleum production begins a steady decline, our entire food system will be strained, testing our ability to feed ourselves.

"How dependent on oil is our food system?" Richard Heinberg, a leading "peak oil" scholar and the author of *The Party's Over: Oil, War and the Fate of Industrial Societies* said in an interview. "Enormously dependent. Fatally dependent, I would say."

Of course, you won't find any oil on your dinner plate, but petroleum and other fossil fuels are inside of every bite you eat. About one-fifth of all U.S. energy use goes into the food system. The synthetic nitrogen fertilizers that are essential for high crop yields are a by-product of natural gas. Gasoline and diesel fuels power the combines that rumble through the grain fields. Countless kilowatts of electricity are burned up in the factories that process all of the packaged goods that line the supermarket shelves. And then there's the gasoline required simply to get food to market. We now have a globalized food system, one in which the typical American meal travels 1,500 miles from farm to fork. Organic products—though they may have a more sustainable veneer—are in many respects no different; 10 percent of organic products come from abroad. Without oil, we would all be on one harsh diet.

About one-fifth of all U.S. energy use goes into the food system.

"We've created an agricultural system where, on average, for every energy of food calorie we produce, we need to expend about 10 calories of fossil fuels," Heinberg said.

Such an imbalance would not be worrisome if there were an inexhaustible supply of oil. But, as every child learns in elementary science class, petroleum is a nonrenewable resource. A heated debate is under way about when that resource will begin to decline. Some say that we have already passed the summit of peak oil and point to a leveling of global petroleum production as proof. The U.S. government argues that we have decades before oil extraction begins to decline. Others calculate that we will hit the peak oil mark sometime in the next 10 years. Regardless of when exactly oil production starts to drop, it's clear that in this century humanity will have to learn to live without cheap, abundant oil.

What this means for our food system is also up for debate. At the very least, costlier oil will lead to more expensive food, especially for processed and packaged goods. At the very worst, peak oil could seriously disrupt agriculture, especially in highly industrialized nations like the United States, where food systems are heavily reliant on oil.

"This era of increasing globalization of our food supply is going to draw to a close here in the next decade or so," Ronnie Cummins, executive director of the Organic Consumers Association, said. "I think it (eventual oil scarcities) is going to mean the end of importing billions of dollars of food from overseas. It's going to mean the end of relatively cheap food in the U.S. And it's going to mean a significant increase in starvation and malnourishment across the world."

Fuel vs. Food

In response to alarms about the fragileness of the food system, some farmers are taking initiatives to wean themselves from petroleum and find more sustainable ways of growing food. One of the most popular approaches is biofuels. For farmers, it's a solution to high oil prices that makes intuitive sense, as it raises the possibility of growers cultivating their own fuel, just as most farmers did a century ago when they harvested oats to feed their horse teams.

There are no simple solutions to agriculture's deep reliance on oil.

Phil Foster is one farmer who has made a commitment to reducing his farm's reliance on fossil fuels. A prominent California organic fruit and vegetable grower who is a supplier to Whole Foods, Foster runs nearly all of the tracks and tractors on his 250-acre farm on B100-pure biodiesel. The remainder of his machines—older tractors with more finicky engines—operate on B30, which is a blend of biodiesel and conventional petroleum diesel. At the same time, Foster is trying to reduce the amount of electricity his farm pays for. Several years ago he installed a bank of solar panels to help power his packing shed, refrigerators, irrigation pumps, and sales office. He calculates that the sun provides about 20 percent of his energy.

For Foster, using biodiesel and employing solar technology isn't just an effort to be environmentally correct. It's simply smart business, he says, a way to ensure that his farm will be economically sustainable over the long run.

"It was kind of a no-brainer for me to move in that direction," Foster said. "Especially in a business like ours, customers that buy organic would tend to like their growers to be kind of on the forefront. As a business that wants to think about longevity, I want to know how we can position ourselves."

Organic growers aren't the only ones bullish on the future of biofuels. Large, conventional grain farmers are also looking at biofuels as a way to reduce their costs, and many corn growers are hoping to make money by selling their surplus harvest to ethanol processors.

[Farming without oil] will likely require a dramatic overhaul of the food system, a wholesale restructuring that would return agriculture to a system of local production for local consumption.

"Diesel fuel used to be a minor cost, but now it's become a major cost," said Paul Penner, who farms 1,000 acres of wheat north of Wichita. "It looks like biodiesel is going to become a long-term solution. So I think we are going to be seeing some bigger switches across the country."

Some people, however, caution that biodiesel is unlikely to evolve into a permanent fix. Though biofuels may be useful in reducing petroleum dependence in the near future, it's doubtful that fuels made from plants could completely unhitch us from oil. Why? For the simple reason that making biofuels requires lots of land, and at some point—were biofuels to become widely popular—the nation would face a choice between growing food and growing fuel.

"As good as it sounds, you're taking crops that initially were being used as a food source and now are being used as fuel sources," said a U.S. Department of Agriculture scientist who asked to remain anonymous. "So where will all the additional food crops come from to feed the demand from American consumers? I expect some problems coming."

Problems involving the trade-off between cultivating food and cultivating fuel are already appearing. According to Ferd Hoefner of the Sustainable Agriculture Coalition, last year farmers in North Dakota sold a large portion of their corn harvest to ethanol processors. But that left local cattle ranchers short of grain to feed their cows, and so they had to import corn from Canada to beef up their herds, corn that was more expensive than the locally grown stuff.

Freewheelin'

As the North Dakota experience shows, there are no simple solutions to agriculture's deep reliance on oil. The fundamental challenge facing farmers—and, by extension, everyone who likes to eat—is how to reduce off-farm inputs and make farms more self-sufficient. That will likely require a dramatic overhaul of the food system, a wholesale restructuring that would return agriculture to a system of local production for local consumption.

"The only good thing about this is that there will be a massive stimulus for rebuilding local and regional food and farming systems, and a big increase in organic and sustainable farms, which are less energy intensive," the Organic Consumer Association's Cummins said.

Amy Courtney is a farmer who is pioneering less energy-intensive ways of farming. Courtney is the owner and sole employee of Freewheelin' Farms, a tiny operation on California's central coast. Four years ago Courtney, 31, started farming by herself on a one-acre plot just a few hundred yards from the Pacific Ocean. On her ocean-view parcel she grows strawberries, blackberries, hothouse tomatoes, cabbage, squash, leeks, and a range of other vegetables. Her produce goes to 16 households in a community supported agriculture (CSA) program and some restaurants in a nearby town, all of which she delivers on her bicycle after a seven-mile ride.

"I was a bike activist and chose not to have a car in my life," Courtney said on a recent sunny afternoon as she stood near the chicken flock that supplies eggs to her CSA members. "Then I got involved with agriculture and saw how much we were spending on diesel and oil spills on the fields, and the whole thing was kind of gross to me. I don't want to support that with my life. Or at least I want to unplug as much as possible. And now, with everything in the Mideast, it's like, duh."

Courtney does use some petroleum. She employs a gasoline-powered rototiller to supplement her hand digging of the soil, and she has a biodiesel truck for hauling manure from a nearby ranch so that she can make her own compost. But she estimates that her farm's annual fuel use is less than 30 gallons. She also tries to be more sustainable by using as many recycled materials as possible. She inherited her greenhouse, and the bike trailer she uses for delivering her produce was scavenged from a junk pile.

"There's stuff out there that people aren't using, including land and equipment," she said. "I'm amazed how much food you can grow on a little piece of land. I don't care if they can't make Pez [a type of candy] as cheap as they used to. I don't care if GM [General Motors] can't keep it together anymore. If we can't feed ourselves, we're f---ed."

Freewheelin' Farms may not be scaled to feed a country of 300 million people. But it is an illustration of the basic principles that will be required to grow food in a post-oil age: muscle-powered, localized, dependent on personal relationships. Courtney's model—in which it takes one person to feed about another 20—also reveals one other change that will likely have to occur with the agricultural system: More people will have to start growing their own food. Currently less than two percent of the U.S. population [is] farmers. If we can no longer rely on the muscle of carbon energy, that number will need to grow.

Author Heinberg says the island nation of Cuba offers a model for how such a transition can occur. After the collapse of the Soviet Union, the Communist nation found itself cut off from the subsidized petroleum it had long depended on. In order to feed itself, the government launched a sweeping program to enlist citizens in urban gardening and composting. In the last decade, the country has become an internationally recognized model of sustainable agriculture.

"[Cuba] basically had an oil famine in the early '90s, and they had to break up the big state-owned farms and start smaller farms," says Heinberg. "They included farming as part of the curriculum in our schools. They raised the salaries of farmers.

"And they had to do these things, or otherwise they simply would not have survived as a society."

The Security of Oil Supply and Demand Is Necessary to Sustain the Global Economy

Ali Hussain

Ali Hussain is an oil consultant and former officer of the Organization of the Petroleum Exporting Countries (OPEC).

"Oil is a fossil fuel, which was formed millions of years ago. Some scientists say that tiny diatoms are the source of oil. Diatoms are sea creatures the size of a pinhead. They can convert sunlight into stored energy. As the diatoms died they fell to the sea floor. Here they were buried under sediment and other rock. The rock squeezed the diatoms and the energy in their bodies could not escape. The carbon eventually turned into oil under great pressure and heat. As the earth changed and moved and folded, pockets where oil and natural gas can be found were formed."

The above definition clearly shows the unique characteristics of oil: how it was formed, the long period it took to materialize and, as a result of such formation, its limited quantity. Consequently oil cannot be reproduced—only replaced with renewed discovery, exploration and development. Therefore, once oil reserves are finished, an oil producer can no longer produce. This is a significant sacrifice to oil producers and a warning to oil consumers to use oil efficiently and stop wasting it. It is estimated that so far the world has produced 400bn [billion] barrels, compared with existing proven oil reserves of 1,200bn barrels. By the end of 2005 Saudi Arabia had produced 111bn barrels, Iran 78bn barrels, Kuwait 37bn barrels, Iraq 32bn barrels and the UAE [United Arab Emirates] 25bn barrels.

Ali Hussain, "Security of Oil Supply and Demand and the Importance of the 'Producer-Consumer' Dialogue," *Middle East Economic Survey*, vol. XLIX, no. 50, December 11, 2006. www.mees.com. Reproduced by permission.

The Importance of Oil

Oil plays an important role in global economic development, providing all the energy for transportation such as cars, trucks, airplanes, etc. It also provides energy inputs such as heating to domestic and industrial buildings as well as lubrication for engines and machines. In addition, oil is a raw material product for plastics, paints, fertilizers, pharmaceuticals, etc. In other words oil is vital for many industries, and modern economies rely heavily on goods and services that contain oil and oil products' elements. According to BP [British Petroleum] data, in 2005 the share of oil as a source of energy in the total world energy mix was about 36.4%. This is compared with other alternative sources of energy such as gas 23.5%, and nuclear (6% each). With regard to renewable sources of energy, hydroelectricity contributed 6% while others such as solar and wind still played a very minor role. Furthermore, the use of these renewable sources, as well as nuclear, is restricted to power generation.

Oil plays an important role in global economic development, providing all the energy for transportation such as cars, trucks, airplanes, etc.

Oil is not a commodity that can be easily replaced by alternative sources. Natural gas and nuclear power cannot compete fully with oil. For example, oil lubricants can only be obtained from oil, and natural gas cannot easily be transported like oil. As for nuclear energy, it continues to suffer from certain safety matters including nuclear waste. And renewable sources of energy have a long way to go before they can significantly compete with oil.

As mentioned earlier, oil is a depletable asset and therefore it is possible that one day in the future the world will be without oil. According to BP statistics, in 2005 the reserves-to-production (R/P) ratio was 40.6 years.

Moreover, due to the importance of oil, all countries in the world, and especially the industrial ones, pay particular attention to the international oil industry and try to encourage their oil and non-oil companies to be involved in the construction and operations of it in two ways:

a. Oil companies, which are engaged in the production of oil and oil products; and

b. Companies, which supply the oil industry with its requirements such as machines, tools, equipments, etc.

Security of Oil Supply

Although oil reserves can be found in many parts of the world, a large proportion of them are concentrated in the Middle East. According to BP data, in 2005 world proven oil reserves were 1,200bn barrels. In the same year OPEC [Organization of the Petroleum Exporting Countries] proven oil reserves were 902bn barrels or 75% of the world total. Furthermore within the Middle East, in 2005, the Gulf's reserves (743bn barrels) accounted for 62% of the world total. This region also enjoys the lowest cost of oil production in the world—in Iraq, for example, about $1-2/B [per barrel].

Due to the importance of oil, one of the most important concerns for oil-consuming countries is the security of oil supplies from the major oil-producing (OPEC) countries. Under the right conditions, these can meet the expected growth in the world oil demand. Currently OPEC meets about 40% of the world oil demand and, as 75% of the world proven oil reserves are located in OPEC countries, these can expand production to meet the anticipated future increase in global demand.

However, in order for OPEC to expand its oil production, it needs to be certain that the oil industry will remain profitable. The industry is capital intensive and OPEC would need to invest billions of dollars in exploration, development, storage, etc., and simultaneously wait 3–10 years to locate and develop these new oil fields before they can become profitable. For example, Khalid al-Falih, a senior vice president in Saudi Aramco, stated in a recent conference in London, that the kingdom planned to invest in the next five years $80bn to increase production to 12mn b/d [12 million barrels per day], expand gas processing facilities and increase refining capacity at home and abroad.

It must be remembered that as OPEC is not the only supplier of oil in the international market, it cannot guarantee oil price stability or the availability of supplies to all oil consumers at all times. To enable OPEC to provide enough investments to increase capacity to meet the expected growth in oil demand, two hurdles must be crossed. They are:

a. Reasonable oil prices in real terms, i.e., taking account of imported inflation and changes of the US dollar exchange rate. According to OPEC data, if 1973 is taken as a base year, due to imported inflation into OPEC countries and the devaluation of the US dollar vis-à-vis other major currencies, the real price of OPEC oil in 2005 was only $10.42/B compared with its nominal price of $50.64/B.

b. Taxation in the major oil-consuming countries. This taxation limits the growth in oil demand and thus reduces the incomes of oil-producing countries, limiting their ability to invest in the growth of their respective production capacities.

Many major industrial countries have introduced heavy taxes on oil products. In some industrial countries, the price that motorists pay for gasoline is three or four times higher than the price of the original crude oil. In some of these countries, taxes account for more than 70% of the final price of oil products. In fact these industrial countries receive much more income from oil taxation than the oil revenues generated by OPEC. According to OPEC data, during 2000–04, the G7 [group of seven industrialized nations including Canada, France, Germany, Italy, Japan, the United Kingdom, and the

United States] countries made a total of $1.6 trillion from oil taxation. This compares with oil revenues of just $1.3 trillion for OPEC countries over the same five-year period. In addition, while the $1.6 trillion in oil tax revenues gathered by the G7 is pure 'profit' this is not the case for the OPEC countries, as the cost of exploring, developing, [and] transporting that oil must be deducted from these revenues.

Major oil producers, such as OPEC countries, need security of demand for their oil.

In addition, such taxation can be considered a transfer of income from oil-exporting to some oil-importing countries. Such income can be used by oil-producing countries in oil exploration and development in order to address the need to increase production capacity as demand rises in the future. If there is not sufficient investment to increase output capacity before it is needed, the international oil market may suffer sudden price shocks. This is essentially what has happened during the last few years. During the last three decades the real price of oil in the international market has been relatively low, as shown earlier, which has discouraged major oil producers, namely OPEC, from increasing production capacity. This in turn led to the stagnation in this capacity at around 31mn b/d and was consequently unable to match the recent significant increase in global oil demand, particularly of light crude, consequently leading to the significant rise in oil prices.

Security of Oil Demand

Major oil producers, such as OPEC countries, need security of demand for their oil. These are developing countries, relying heavily on the income from oil exports (i.e., oil revenues) in foreign currencies, which they use to import the goods and services they require for their development. In some oil-producing countries oil exports account for more than 90% of total exports. Thus, any drastic reduction in the demand for oil, and hence oil exports and oil revenues, may have significant economic as well as political impact on these countries.

Oil-producing countries will be reluctant to embark on major oil production capacity expansion if oil consumers intend in the future to substitute oil with other sources of energy and plan to increase taxation on oil products. In its recent report *World Energy Outlook 2006*, the IEA [International Energy Agency, an international forum on energy security] stated, for environmental and political security reasons, "the world is on a course that will lead it 'from crisis to crisis' unless governments act immediately to save energy and invest in nuclear and biofuels." In addition, in major industrial countries some writers advocate further increases in taxation on oil products. For example, in a recent article in the *Los Angeles Times*, Steven Mufson recommended: "A sharp hike in energy taxes on petrol and other fossil fuels would not only help improve the government's balance sheet, but it would also be a way to start addressing global warming." Furthermore, every now and then, mainly for political reasons, reports published in major oil-consuming countries, particularly the US, advocate an "Independent Energy Policy," which usually recommends reducing these countries' dependence on Middle East oil. Such reports and statements cannot and will not encourage major oil producers in the Middle East to increase oil production capacity significantly. Such important issues must not be left to the issuance of reports and statements, but be discussed thoroughly in direct dialogue between consumers and producers.

As mentioned above, the oil industry is capital intensive and requires a considerable amount of investments to explore, develop and produce oil, as well as to maintain production capacity and facilities. Therefore oil producers like OPEC countries have to earn reasonable returns on their investments to be able to continue to pursue these operations. It has been estimated that in the past it cost Saudi Arabia \$2bn annually to keep its surplus production capacity.

A reduction in oil demand will force oil production to slow down or even stop. This in turn may damage some oil fields and could reduce the amount of oil that can be recovered from them in the future.

A reduction in oil demand and a decline in oil-producing countries' oil exports and revenues may force these countries to reduce their investments in the oil industry itself for two reasons:

1. The reduction in the money available for investments; and
2. There will be fewer incentives to expand future production capacity.

Under such conditions the world could face a shortage in oil supplies, which would have negative effects on the global economy. To avoid these problems oil-producing countries must be assured of reasonable oil prices in real terms (i.e., taking imported inflation and the devaluation of the US dollar into consideration) and stable growth in oil demand. This will help them maintain their production levels and provide enough investments for future growth in oil production capacity to meet future growth in world demand. Due to the relatively low real price of OPEC oil during the last two decades, new and existing oil fields have faced lower levels of investments resulting in OPEC's production capacity, particularly Saudi Arabia's, to remain static. Given that the majority of OPEC countries are producing at or near full capacity levels to meet the recent increase in oil demand, the surplus production capacity in these countries, especially in Saudi Arabia, has declined to only 1.5mn b/d mostly of heavy crude oil. Thus, the ability of OPEC countries to meet the anticipated ongoing growth in oil demand will be limited unless more money is invested in their oil industries.

Obviously the security of oil supplies depends heavily on the security of oil demand. To ensure the security of both supply and demand, oil producers and oil consumers must work together.

Oil Producers–Oil Consumers Dialogue

According to the IEA, the global demand for oil is expected to increase from the present level of 84mn b/d to 116mn b/d in 2030. With their large oil reserves, some countries in the Middle East, particularly in the Gulf region, will be able to meet such extra demand. These countries include Iraq, Saudi Arabia, Iran, Kuwait and the UAE—the future "Mini-OPEC" countries. Oil-consumer countries must be prepared to negotiate with them from "now" on future oil supplies. To leave it until later will be "too late."

The global demand for oil is expected to increase from the present level of 84mn b/d [barrels per day] to 116mn b/d in 2030.

A Dialogue About Oil

As oil is an important strategic global commodity and affects daily life everywhere, major oil-producing countries must take the lead in organizing an effective and useful dialogue with oil consumers. Such a dialogue should also include minor oil consumers and producers, as well as international oil companies, which play a major role in the global oil industry.

This dialogue must concentrate its efforts to discuss important matters related to oil, which affect the lives of all people worldwide. Subjects to be discussed can include:

- International oil prices and their effect on the world economy.

- The effect of oil usage on the environment.

- Present and future investments in the international oil industry.

- The purchasing power of oil revenues of oil exports.

- Taxation on certain oil products in major oil consuming countries.

- Security of oil supply and security of oil demand.

There have been some international conferences and seminars covering oil producers–consumers dialogue. Furthermore, the International Energy Forum (IEF) has recently been established in Saudi Arabia to deal with this issue. This is the right forum for consumers and producers to meet and discuss the above matters and must therefore be supported. However, so far the dialogue issue is not being taken seriously enough and unless there are comprehensive discussions and scientific studies of all the key subjects, with an effective mechanism established to implement the findings of these discussions, studies and possible agreements, then all valuable efforts will unfortunately be wasted.

It is . . . in the interest of all oil producers, oil consumers, international oil companies and future generations to see that oil is produced, priced and used . . . for the benefit of all.

The establishment of the IEF is a good example of the intention of major oil-producing countries to play a vital role in this dialogue and tackle all related issues. Oil producers have not only an economic but also a moral obligation to provide enough oil supplies to consumers. It is also in their interests to increase production and hence exports to increase their oil revenues, which they can use to develop their economies. It is also in the interest of all oil producers, oil consumers, international oil companies and future generations to see that oil is produced, priced and used in a scientific and efficient way for the benefit of all.

Finally, major oil producers and consumers must remember that oil is a strategic commodity: Its quantity is limited, and because it is so vital for daily life everywhere, it must be considered very seriously. It is their obligation and duty to adopt policies that will bring benefits not only to their nations, but also to the international community at large. It is high time oil consumers and producers stopped adopting short-term policies and started following and implementing long-term ones.

The United States Must Unleash a New Clean Energy Economy

Barack Obama

Barack Obama is the forty-fourth president of the United States.

Roughly a century and a half ago, in the late [1850s], the Seneca Oil Company hired an unemployed train conductor named Edwin Drake to investigate the oil springs of Titusville, Pennsylvania. Around this time, oil was literally bubbling up from the ground—but nobody knew what to do with it. It had limited economic value and often all it did was ruin crops or pollute drinking water.

Now, people were starting to refine oil for use as a fuel. Collecting oil remained time consuming, though, and it was backbreaking, and it was costly; it wasn't efficient, as workers harvested what they could find in the shallow ground—they'd literally scoop it up. But Edwin Drake had a plan. He purchased a steam engine, and he built a derrick, and he began to drill.

And months passed. And progress was slow. The team managed to drill into the bedrock just a few feet each day. And crowds gathered and they mocked Mr. Drake. They thought [he] and the other diggers were foolish. The well that they were digging even earned the nickname "Drake's Folly." But Drake wouldn't give up. And he had an advantage: total desperation. It had to work. And then one day, it finally did.

One morning, the team returned to the creek to see crude oil rising up from beneath the surface. And soon, Drake's well was producing what was then an astonishing amount of oil—perhaps 10, 20 barrels every day. And then speculators fol-

Barack Obama, "Remarks by the President on Clean Energy, Newton Iowa," The White House, Office of the Press Secretary, April 22, 2009.

lowed and they built similar rigs as far as the eye could see. In the next decade, the area would produce tens of millions of barrels of oil. And as the industry grew, so did the ingenuity of those who sought to profit from it, as competitors developed new techniques to drill and transport oil to drive down costs and gain a competitive advantage in the marketplace.

America has always led the world in producing and harnessing new forms of energy.

Now, our history is filled with such stories—stories of daring talent, of dedication to an idea even when the odds are great, of the unshakable belief that in America, all things are possible.

And this has been especially true in energy production. From the first commercially viable steamboat developed by Robert Fulton to the first modern solar cell developed at Bell Labs; from the experiments of Benjamin Franklin to harness the energy of lightning to the experiments of Enrico Fermi to harness the power contained in the atom, America has always led the world in producing and harnessing new forms of energy.

A New Era of Energy Exploration

But just as we've led the global economy in developing new sources of energy, we've also led in consuming energy. While we make up less than 5 percent of the world's population, we produce roughly a quarter of the world's demand for oil.

And this appetite comes now at a tremendous cost to our economy. It's the cost measured by our trade deficit; 20 percent of what we spend on imports is the price of our oil imports. We send billions of dollars overseas to oil-exporting nations, and I think all of you know many of them are not our friends. It's the same costs attributable to our vulnerability to the volatility of oil markets. Every time the world oil market goes up, you're getting stuck at the pump. It's the cost we feel in shifting weather patterns that are already causing record-breaking droughts, unprecedented wildfires, more intense storms.

It's a cost we've known ever since the gas shortages of the 1970s. And yet, for more than 30 years, too little has been done about it. There's a lot of talk of action when oil prices skyrocket like they did last summer [2008] and everybody says [we've] got to do something about energy independence, but then it slips from the radar when oil prices start falling like they have recently. So we shift from shock to indifference time and again, year after year.

We can't afford that approach anymore—not when the cost for our economy, for our country, and for our planet is so high. So on this Earth Day [April 22, 2009], it is time for us to lay a new foundation for economic growth by beginning a new era of energy exploration in America. That's why I'm here.

Now, the choice we face is not between saving our environment and saving our economy. The choice we face is between prosperity and decline. We can remain the world's leading importer of oil, or we can become the world's leading exporter of clean energy. We can allow climate change to wreak unnatural havoc across the landscape, or we can create jobs working to prevent its worst effects. We can hand over the jobs of the 21st century to our competitors, or we can confront what countries in Europe and Asia have already recognized as both a challenge and an opportunity: The nation that leads the world in creating new energy sources will be the nation that leads the 21st-century global economy.

America can be that nation. America must be that nation. And while we seek new forms of fuel to power our homes and cars and businesses, we will rely on the same ingenuity—the same American spirit—that has always been a part of our American story.

Now, this will not be easy. There aren't any silver bullets. There's no magic energy source right now. Maybe some kid in a lab somewhere is figuring it out. Twenty years from now, there may be an entirely new energy source that we don't yet know about. But right now, there's no silver bullet. It's going to take a variety of energy sources, pursued through a variety of policies, to drastically reduce our dependence on oil and fossil fuels. As I've often said, in the short term, as we transition to renewable energy, we can and should increase our domestic production of oil and natural gas. We're not going to transform our economy overnight. We still need more oil, we still need more gas. If we've got some here in the United States that we can use, we should find it and do so in an environmentally sustainable way. We also need to find safer ways to use nuclear power and store nuclear waste.

But the bulk of our efforts must focus on unleashing a new, clean-energy economy that will begin to reduce our dependence on foreign oil, will cut our carbon pollution by about 80 percent by 2050, and create millions of new jobs right here in America—right here in Newton [Iowa].

Energy Efficiency

My administration has already taken unprecedented action towards this goal. It's work that begins with the simplest, fastest, most effective way we have to make our economy cleaner, and that is to make our economy more energy efficient. . . .

Through the American Recovery and Reinvestment Act, we've begun to modernize 75 percent of all federal building space, which has the potential to reduce long-term energy costs just in federal buildings by billions of dollars on behalf of taxpayers. We're providing grants to states to help weatherize hundreds of thousands of homes, which will save the families that benefit about $350 each year. That's like a $350 tax cut.

Consumers are also eligible as part of the Recovery Act for up to $1,500 in tax credits to purchase more efficient cooling and heating systems, insulation and windows in order to reduce their energy bills. And I've issued a memorandum to the Department of Energy to implement more aggressive efficiency standards for common household appliances, like dishwashers and refrigerators. We actually have made so much progress, just on something as simple as refrigerators, that you have seen refrigerators today many times more efficient than they were back in 1974. We save huge amounts of energy if we upgrade those appliances. Through this—through these steps—over the next three decades, we will save twice the amount of energy produced by all the coal-fired power plants in America in any given year.

Even as we're conserving energy, we need to change the way we produce energy.

We're already seeing reports from across the country of how this is beginning to create jobs, because local governments and businesses rush to hire folks to do the work of building and installing these energy-efficient products.

And these steps will spur job creation and innovation as more Americans make purchases that place a premium on reducing energy consumption. Businesses across the country will join the competition, developing new products, seeking new consumers.

In the end, the sum total of choices made by consumers and companies in response to our recovery plan will mean less pollution in our air and water, it'll reduce costs for families and businesses—money in your pocket—and it will lower our overall reliance on fossil fuels, which disrupt our environment and endanger our children's future.

So, that's step number one: energy efficiency. That's the low-hanging fruit. But energy efficiency can only take us part of the way. Even as we're conserving energy, we need to change the way we produce energy.

Clean Energy

Today, America produces less than 3 percent of our electricity through renewable sources like wind and solar—less than 3 percent. Now, in comparison, Denmark produces almost 20 percent of their electricity through wind power. We pioneered solar technology, but we've fallen behind countries like Germany and Japan in generating it, even though we've got more sun than either country.

I don't accept this is the way it has to be. When it comes to renewable energy, I don't think we should be followers, I think it's time for us to lead.

We are now poised to do exactly that. According to some estimates, last year, 40 percent of all new generating capacity in our country came from wind. In Iowa, you know what this means. This state is second only to Texas in installed wind capacity, which more than doubled last year alone. The result: Once shuttered factories are whirring back to life right here at Trinity [Structural Towers, a manufacturer of the towers on which wind turbines sit]; at TPI Composites, where more than 300 workers are manufacturing turbine blades, same thing; elsewhere in this state and across America.

In 2000, energy technology represented just one half of one percent of all venture capital investments. Today, it's more than 10 percent.

The recovery plan seeks to build on this progress, and encourage even faster growth. We're providing incentives to double our nation's capacity to generate renewable energy over the next few years—extending the production tax credit, providing loan guarantees, offering grants to spur investment in new sources of renewable fuel and electricity.

My budget also invests $15 billion each year for 10 years to develop clean energy, including wind power and solar power, geothermal energy and clean coal technology.

And today I'm announcing that my administration is taking another historic step. Through the Department of Interior, we are establishing a program to authorize—for the very first time—the leasing of federal waters for projects to generate electricity from wind as well as from ocean currents and other renewable sources. And this will open the door to major investments in offshore clean energy. For example, there is enormous interest in wind projects off the coasts of New Jersey and Delaware, and today's announcement will enable these projects to move forward.

It's estimated that if we fully pursue our potential for wind energy on land and offshore, wind can generate as much as 20 percent of our electricity by 2030 and create a quarter-million jobs in the process—250,000 jobs in the process, jobs that pay well and provide good benefits. It's a win-win: It's good for the environment; it's great for the economy.

We have to create the incentives for companies to develop the next generation of clean-energy vehicles—and for Americans to drive them.

Even as we pursue renewable energy from the wind and the sun and other sources, we also need a smarter, stronger electricity grid—some of you have been hearing about this, this smart grid—a grid that can carry energy from one end of this country to the other. So when you guys are building these amazing towers and the turbines are going up and they're producing energy, we've got to make sure that energy produced in Iowa can get to Chicago; energy produced in North Dakota can get to Milwaukee. That's why we're making an $11 billion investment through the recovery plan to modernize the way we distribute electricity.

Clean-Energy Vehicles

And as we're taking unprecedented steps to save energy and generate new kinds of energy for our homes and businesses, we need to do the same for our cars and trucks. . . .

We have to create the incentives for companies to develop the next generation of clean-energy vehicles—and for Americans to drive them, particularly as the U.S. auto industry moves forward on a historic restructuring that can position it for a more prosperous future.

And that's why my administration has begun to put in place higher fuel economy standards for the first time since the mid-1980s, so our cars will get better mileage, saving drivers money, spurring companies to develop more innovative products. The Recovery Act also includes $2 billion in competitive grants to develop the next generation of batteries for plug-in hybrids. We're planning to buy 17,600 American-made, fuel-efficient cars and trucks for the government fleet. And today, Vice President [Joe] Biden is announcing a Clean Cities grant program through the Recovery Act to help state and local governments purchase clean-energy vehicles, too.

We can clean up our environment and put people back to work in a strong U.S. auto industry, but we've got to have some imagination and we've got to be bold. We can't be looking backwards, we've got to look—we've got to look forward.

My budget is also making unprecedented investments in mass transit, high-speed rail, and in our highway system to reduce the congestion that wastes money and time and energy. We need to connect Des Moines to Chicago with high-speed rail all across the Midwest. That way you don't have to take off your shoes when you want to go visit Chicago going through the airport.

My budget also invests in advanced biofuels and ethanol, which, as I've said, is an important transitional fuel to help us end our dependence on foreign oil while moving towards clean, homegrown sources of energy.

And while we're creating the incentives for companies to develop these technologies, we're also creating incentives for consumers to adapt to these new technologies. So the Recovery Act includes a new credit—new tax credit for up to $7,500 to encourage Americans to buy more fuel-efficient cars and trucks. So if you guys are in the market to buy a car or truck, check out that tax credit.

In addition, innovation depends on innovators doing the research and testing the ideas that might not pay off in the short run—some of them will be dead-ends, won't pay off at all—but when taken together, hold incredible potential over the long term. And that's why my recovery plan includes the largest investment in basic research funding in American history. And my budget includes a 10-year commitment to make the Research and Experimentation Tax Credit permanent. That's a tax credit that returns $2 to the economy for every dollar we spend. That young guy in the garage designing a new engine or a new battery, that computer scientist who's imagining a new way of thinking about energy, we need to fund them now, fund them early, because that's what America has always been about: technology and innovation.

Addressing Climate Change

And this is only the beginning. My administration will be pursuing comprehensive legislation to move towards energy independence and prevent the worst consequences of climate change, while creating the incentives to make clean energy the profitable kind of energy in America.

Now, there's been some debate about this whole climate change issue. But it's serious. It could be a problem. It could end up having an impact on farmers. . . . If you're starting to see temperatures grow—rise 1, 2, 3 percent, have a profound impact on our lives. And the fact is, we place limits on pollutants like sulfur dioxide and nitrogen dioxide and other harmful emissions. But we haven't placed any limits on carbon dioxide and other greenhouse gases. It's what's called the carbon loophole.

Now, last week, in response to a mandate from the United States Supreme Court, the Environmental Protection Agency determined that carbon dioxide and other tailpipe emissions are harmful to the health and well-being of our people. So there's no question that we have to regulate carbon pollution in some way; the only question is how we do it.

I believe the best way to do it is through legislation that places a market-based cap on these kinds of emissions. And today, key members of my administration are testifying in Congress on a bill that seeks to enact exactly this kind of market-based approach. My hope is that this will be the vehicle through which we put this policy in effect.

And here's how a market-based cap would work: We'd set a cap, a ceiling, on all the carbon dioxide and other greenhouse gases that our economy is allowed to produce in total, combining the emissions from cars and trucks, coal-fired power plants, energy-intensive industries, all sources.

[Climate change] is also a global problem, so it's going to require a global coalition to solve it.

And by setting an overall cap, carbon pollution becomes like a commodity. It places a value on a limited resource, and that is the ability to pollute. And to determine that value, just like any other traded commodity, we'd create a market where companies could buy and sell the right to produce a certain amount of carbon pollution. And in this way, every company can determine for itself whether it makes sense to spend the money to become cleaner or more efficient, or to spend the money on a certain amount of allowable pollution.

Over time, as the cap on greenhouse gases is lowered, the commodity becomes scarcer—and the price goes up. And year by year, companies and consumers would have greater incentive to invest in clean energy and energy efficiency as the price of the status quo became more expensive.

What this does is it makes wind power more economical, makes solar power more economical. Clean energy all becomes more economical. And by closing the carbon loophole through this kind of market-based cap, we can address in a systematic way all the facets of the energy crisis: We lower our dependence on foreign oil, we reduce our use of fossil fuels, we promote new industries right here in America. We set up the right incentives so that everybody is moving in the same direction towards energy independence. . . .

Now, this is also a global problem, so it's going to require a global coalition to solve it. If we've got problems with climate change, and the temperature rising all around the world, that knows no boundaries; and the decisions of any nation will affect every nation. So next week, I will be gathering leaders of major economies from all around the world to talk about how we can work together to address this energy crisis and this climate crisis.

Truth is the United States has been slow to participate in this kind of a process, working with other nations. But those days are over now. We are ready to engage—and we're asking other nations to join us in tackling this challenge together. . . .

I'm confident that we can be and will be the benefactors of a brighter future for our children and grandchildren. That can be our legacy—a legacy of vehicles powered by clean renewable energy traveling past newly opened factories; of industries employing millions of Americans in the work of protecting our planet; of an economy exporting the energy of the future instead of importing the energy of the past; of a nation once again leading the world to meet the challenges of our time.

Sustainability Is the Next Phase of Human Development

Eric McLamb

Eric McLamb is founder and president of Ecology Global Network, a Web site that provides news and information about the environment.

The Industrial Revolution marked a major turning point in Earth's ecology and humans' relationship with their environment. As the Industrial Revolution dramatically changed every aspect of human life and lifestyles ... from human development, health and life longevity, to social improvements ... its human impact on natural resources, public health, energy usage and sanitation would not begin to register in the world's psyche until the early 1960s, some 200 years after its beginnings.

It wasn't that the Industrial Revolution became a stalwart juggernaut overnight. It started in the mid-1700s in Great Britain when machinery began to replace manual labor and fossil fuels replaced wind, water, and wood primarily for the manufacture of textiles and the development of iron-making processes. The full impact of the Industrial Revolution would not begin to be realized until about 100 years later in the 1800s when the use of machines to replace human labor spread throughout Europe, North America and the rest of the world. This transformation is referred to as the industrialization of the world ... processes that gave rise to sweeping increases in production capacity and would affect all basic human needs, including food production, medicine, housing, and clothing. Not only did society develop the ability to have more things quicker, it would be able to develop better things. These industrialization processes continue today.

Eric McLamb, "The Industrial Revolution and Its Impact on Our Environment," Ecology Global Network, May 19, 2008. http://ecology.com. © 2008 ecology.com. Reproduced by permission

The Industrial Revolution and Population Growth

The most prolific evidence of the Industrial Revolution's impact on the modern world can be seen in the worldwide human population growth. Modern humans have been around for about 2.2 million years. By the dawn of the first millennium A.D., estimates place the total world human population at between 150–200 million, and 300 million in the year 1,000 (a little less than the population of the United States today). The world human population growth rate would be about .1 percent (.001) per year for the next seven to eight centuries.

Exponential population growth led to the exponential requirements for resources, energy, food, housing and land as well as the exponential increase in waste by-products.

In another 750 years, at the dawn of the Industrial Revolution in the mid 1700s, the world's human population grew about another 57% to 700 million and would see one billion in 1800. The birth of the Industrial Revolution would alter medicine and living standards resulting in the population explosion that would commence at that point and steamroll into the 20th and 21st centuries. In only 100 years after the onset of the Industrial Revolution, the world population would grow 100 percent to two billion people in 1927 (about 1.6 billion by 1900).

During the 20th century, the world population would take on exponential proportions, growing to six billion people just before the start of the 21st century. That's a 400% population increase in a single century. Since the beginnings of the Industrial Revolution to today—in about 250 years—the world human population has increased by six billion people!

Human population growth is indelibly tied together with increased use of natural and man-made resources, energy, land for growing food and for living, and waste by-products that are disposed to decompose, pollute or be recycled. Naturally, the exponential population growth led to the exponential requirements for resources, energy, food, housing and land as well as the exponential increase in waste by-products.

It will take time, continued ingenuity and vast economic incentives to transform dependence on [fossil fuels] ... that fostered the growth and prosperity launched by the Industrial Revolution.

Awakening to the Implications of Unsustainable Growth and Dependence on Limited Resources

There were many indicators that the Industrial Revolution had propelled the world human population into an era of living and production at the ultimate expense of the human condition and the resources that were (and could be) taken for granted for the entire prior history of humankind. There were always more resources than the demand for them. Yet, it would take one person in the 1960s to make the general public aware of the cause and effect of human outgrowth from the Industrial Revolution. Rachel Carson took on the powerful and robust chemical industry in her globally acclaimed 1962 book, *Silent Spring*, and raised important questions about humans' impact on nature. For the first time, the public and industry would begin to grasp the concept of sustainable production and development.

It was the fossil fuel coal that fueled the Industrial Revolution, forever changing the way people would live and utilize energy. While this propelled human progress to extraordinary levels, it came at extraordinary costs to our environment and ultimately the health of all living things. And while coal and other fossil fuels were also taken for granted as being inexhaustible, it was American geophysicist M. King Hubbert who predicted in 1949 that the fossil fuel era would be very short-lived and that other energy sources would need to be relied upon.

Hubbert predicted that fossil fuel production, in particular oil, would reach its peak starting in 1970 and would go into steady decline against the rising energy demands of the population. Just like that, the decline in production started in the United States in 1971 and has spread to other oil-producing nations as well. This peak production is known as "Hubbert's peak." By the time the world began to heed Hubbert's prediction, the use of fossil fuels—so heavily relied upon to fuel the Industrial Revolution—had become so firmly interwoven into human progress and economy that changing this energy system would drastically alter the very way we have lived our lives. It will happen, but it will take time, continued ingenuity and vast economic incentives to transform dependence on this fuel that fostered the growth and prosperity launched by the Industrial Revolution.

We will enter a new era of sustainability. That is the next revolution.

Looking back at the beginning of the Industrial Revolution, it is difficult to realize how what took place then is having such complicated and vast effects today, but that is the principle of environmental unity—a change in one system will cause changes in others. Certainly, the seeds of progress—and the ramifications of that progress—were planted then. And with the very same mechanisms and effects that brought about both the progress and the indelibly connected results of that progress to our ecology—the good, the bad and the ugly—over the last 250 years, we will enter a new era of sustainability. That is the next revolution.

Organizations to Contact

The editors have compiled the following list of organizations concerned with the issues debated in this book. The descriptions are derived from materials provided by the organizations. All have publications or information available for interested readers. The list was compiled on the date of publication of the present volume; the information provided here may change. Be aware that many organizations take several weeks or longer to respond to inquiries, so allow as much time as possible.

Cato Institute
1000 Massachusetts Avenue NW
Washington, DC   20001-5403
(202) 842-0200 • fax: (202) 842-3490
Web site: www.cato.org

The Cato Institute is a nonprofit public policy research foundation that promotes a libertarian point of view that emphasizes principles of limited government, free markets, individual liberty, and peace. One of the Cato Institute's research areas is energy and the environment. The institute is committed to protecting the environment without sacrificing economic liberty and believes that those goals are mutually supporting, not mutually exclusive. Recent publications include *Cap-and-Trade Is Dead. Long Live Cap-and-Trade* and *The Case Against Government Intervention in Energy Markets*.

Energy Information Administration (EIA)
1000 Independence Avenue SW, Washington, DC   20585
(202) 586-8800
e-mail: InfoCtr@eia.doe.gov
Web site: www.eia.doe.gov

The Energy Information Administration (EIA) is the statistical agency of the U.S. Department of Energy (DOE) and is the nation's main source of unbiased energy data, analysis, and forecasting. Its mission is to provide policy-neutral data, forecasts, and analyses to promote sound policy making, efficient markets, and public understanding regarding energy and its interaction with the economy and the environment. The EIA Web site is a source of various reports and publications such as *Petroleum Supply Monthly, Monthly Energy Review*, the *Annual Energy Review*, the *Short-Term Energy Outlook*, and the *Annual Energy Outlook*.

Environmental Literacy Council

1625 K Street NW, Suite 1020, Washington, DC 20006-3868
(202) 296-0390 • fax: (202) 822-0991
e-mail: info@enviroliteracy.org
Web site: www.enviroliteracy.org

The Environmental Literacy Council is an independent organization that helps teachers, students, policy makers, and the public find cross-disciplinary resources on the environment. The council offers free background information on common environmental science concepts; vetted resources to broaden understanding; and curricular materials that give teachers the tools to augment their own backgrounds on environmental issues. The Web site contains a section on energy that provides information, recommended resources, and lesson plans relating to petroleum and U.S. energy policies.

Institute for the Study of Energy and Our Future (ISEOF)

PO Box 270762, Fort Collins, CO 80527-0762
Web site: www.theoildrum.com

The Institute for the Study of Energy and Our Future (ISEOF) is a nonprofit corporation that publishes The Oil Drum, a Web site that facilitates civil, evidence-based discussions about energy and its impact on our future. According to the Web site, the world is near the point at which new oil production cannot keep up with increased energy demand and the depletion of older oil fields, resulting in a decline of total world oil production. The Web site is a source of analysis, research, and discussion of energy-related topics such as peak oil, sustainable development and growth, and the implications of these ideas on politics.

International Energy Agency (IEA)

9 rue de la Fédération, Paris Cedex 15   75739
  France
+33 140576500/01 • fax: +33 140576559
e-mail: info@iea.org
Web site: www.iea.org

The International Energy Agency (IEA) is an intergovernmental organization that acts as energy policy advisor to twenty-eight member countries in their effort to ensure reliable, affordable, and clean energy for their citizens. Founded during the oil crisis of 1973–74, the IEA's initial role was to coordinate measures in times of oil supply emergencies, but that mandate has broadened to include promoting energy security, economic development, and environmental protection. The IEA's current work focuses on climate change policies, market reform, energy technology collaboration, and outreach to major consumers and producers of energy, such as China, India, Russia, and the nations of OPEC (Organization of the Petroleum Exporting Countries). Publications available from IEA include topics such as *Energy Technology Transitions for Industry* and *Transport, Energy and CO_2: Moving Towards Sustainability.*

Natural Resources Defense Council (NRDC)

40 West Twentieth Street, New York, NY   10011
(212) 727-2700 • fax: (212) 727-1773
e-mail: nrdcinfo@nrdc.org
Web site: www.nrdc.org

Founded in 1970, the Natural Resources Defense Council (NRDC) is one of the nation's oldest environmental advocacy organizations. With a staff of more than three hundred lawyers, scientists, and policy experts, NRDC works to protect the planet's wildlife and wild places and to ensure a safe and healthy environment for all living things. Among the issues on NRDC's agenda are curbing global warming, getting toxic chemicals out of the environment, moving America beyond oil, reviving our oceans, saving wildlife and wild places, and helping China go green. The group publishes a monthly newsletter, and the NRDC Web site is a good source of information about clean energy options and green living.

Pew Center on Global Climate Change

2102 Wilson Boulevard, Suite 550, Arlington, VA   22201
(703) 516-4146 • fax: (703) 841-1422
Web site: www.pewclimate.org

The Pew Center on Global Climate Change was established in 1998 as a nonprofit, nonpartisan, independent organization whose mission is to provide credible information, straight answers, and innovative solutions in the effort to address global climate change. The Pew Center seeks to provide a forum for objective research and analysis and for the development of pragmatic policies and solutions. The center's Web site is an excellent source of publications, reports, fact sheets, articles, and speeches on all facets of the energy/climate change issue.

Post Carbon Institute

613 Fourth Street, Suite 208, Santa Rosa, CA   95404
(707) 823-8700 • fax: (866) 797-5820
Web site: www.postcarbon.org

The Post Carbon Institute is a nonprofit organization that helps individuals and communities understand and respond to the environmental, societal, and economic crises created by our dependence on fossil fuels. The group believes that world oil production has peaked, and it aims to facilitate the process of transitioning to a more sustainable, post-carbon world. The group publishes a monthly *Post Carbon Newsletter*, featuring the latest news and information, and its Web site is a good source of articles, commentaries, reports, and books relating to oil depletion and the future of oil, energy, and the economy.

Resources for the Future (RFF)
1616 P Street NW, Suite 600, Washington, DC   20036
(202)328-5000 • fax: (202)939-3460
Web site: www.rff.org

Resources for the Future (RFF) is a nonprofit, nonpartisan organization that conducts independent research—rooted primarily in economics and other social sciences—on environmental, energy, natural resource, and public health issues. RFF was created at the recommendation of William S. Paley, then head of the Columbia Broadcasting System (CBS), who had chaired a presidential commission that examined whether the United States was becoming overly dependent on foreign sources of important natural resources and commodities. Today one of the group's main areas of focus is energy and climate change. Examples of RFF publications include *An Economic Assessment of Eliminating Oil and Gas Company Tax Preferences* and *The Challenge of Climate for Energy Markets.*

U.S. Department of Energy (DOE)
1000 Independence Avenue SW, Washington, DC   20585
(202)586-5000 • fax: (202)586-4403
Web site: www.energy.gov

The U.S. Department of Energy (DOE) is the main federal agency responsible for advancing the national, economic, and energy security of the United States. The DOE works to achieve energy and nuclear security; to strengthen U.S. scientific discovery and economic competitiveness; and to protect the environment. The DOE Web site is a useful source of information about issues such as America's readiness to respond to oil disruptions and the national Strategic Petroleum Reserve.

World Energy Council
5th Floor, Regency House, 1–4 Warwick Street
London   W1B 5LT
   United Kingdom
+44 2077345996 • fax: +44 2077345926

e-mail: info@worldenergy.org
Web site: www.worldenergy.org

The World Energy Council (WEC) is the foremost multi-energy organization in the world today. WEC has member committees in nearly one hundred countries, including most of the largest energy-producing and energy-consuming countries. Established in 1923, the organization's mission is to promote the sustainable supply and use of energy around the world. Examples of WEC publications include *Assessment of Energy Policy and Practices*, *Energy Efficiency Policies*, and *Europe's Vulnerability to Energy Crisis*.

Bibliography

Books

Duncan Clarke — *The Battle for Barrels: Peak Oil Myths & World Oil Futures.* London: Profile Books, 2007.

Kenneth S. Deffeyes — *Beyond Oil: The View from Hubbert's Peak.* New York: Hill & Wang, 2006.

Kenneth S. Deffeyes — *Hubbert's Peak: The Impending World Oil Shortage.* Princeton, NJ: Princeton University Press, 2008.

Alan Greenspan — *The Age of Turbulence: Adventures in a New World.* New York: Penguin, 2007.

Richard Heinberg — *Blackout: Coal, Climate and the Last Energy Crisis.* Gabriola Island, BC, Canada: New Society Publishers, 2009.

Richard Heinberg — *The Party's Over: Oil, War and the Fate of Industrial Societies.* Gabriola Island, BC, Canada: New Society Publishers, 2005.

Antonia Juhasz — *The Tyranny of Oil: The World's Most Powerful Industry—and What We Must Do to Stop It.* New York: Harper Paperbacks, 2009.

Michael T. Klare — *Blood and Oil: The Dangers and Consequences of America's Growing Dependency on Imported Petroleum.* New York: Holt, 2005.

James Howard Kunstler — *The Long Emergency: Surviving the End of Oil, Climate Change, and Other Converging Catastrophes of the Twenty-First Century.* New York: Grove Press, 2006.

Gal Luft and Anne Korin, eds. — *Energy Security Challenges for the 21st Century: A Reference Handbook.* Santa Barbara, CA: Praeger Security International, 2009.

Lisa Margonelli — *Oil on the Brain: Petroleum's Long, Strange Trip to Your Tank.* New York: Broadway, 2008.

Leonardo Maugeri — *The Age of Oil: What They Don't Want You to Know About the World's Most Controversial Resource.* Guilford, CT: The Lyons Press, 2007.

Robin M. Mills — *The Myth of the Oil Crisis: Overcoming the Challenges of Depletion, Geopolitics, and Global Warming.* Westport, CT: Praeger, 2008.

Paul Roberts — *The End of Oil: On the Edge of a Perilous New World.* New York: Mariner Books, 2005.

Jeff Rubin — *Why Your World Is About to Get a Whole Lot Smaller: Oil and the End of Globalization.* New York: Random House, 2009.

Sonia Shah — *Crude: The Story of Oil.* New York: Seven Stories Press, 2006.

Matthew R. Simmons — *Twilight in the Desert: The Coming Saudi Oil Shock and the World Economy.* Hoboken, NJ: Wiley, 2006.

Christopher Steiner — *$20 Per Gallon: How the Inevitable Rise in the Price of Gasoline Will Change Our Lives for the Better.* New York: Grand Central Publishing, 2009.

Daniel Yergin — *The Prize: The Epic Quest for Oil, Money and Power.* New York: Free Press, 2008.

Periodicals

Christopher Beddor, Winny Chen, Rudy deLeon, Shiyong Park, and Daniel J. Weiss — "Securing America's Future: Enhancing Our National Security by Reducing Oil Dependence and Environmental Damage," Center for American Progress, August 2009. www.americanprogress.org.

John Dillin — "Before the Oil Runs Out: How Will This Era End?" *Christian Science Monitor,* September 20, 2005. www.csmonitor.com.

Humberto Fontova	"Offshore Oil Drilling: An Environmental Bonanza," *American Thinker*, April 28, 2009. www.americanthinker.com.
Thomas L. Friedman	"Addicted to Oil," *New York Times*, June 22, 2008. www.nytimes.com.
Dominic Frisby	"Why the Rising Oil Price Isn't Bad News for Stocks," *MoneyWeek*, June 22, 2009. www.moneyweek.com.
Russell Gold and Ann Davis	"Oil Officials See Limit Looming on Production," *Wall Street Journal*, November 19, 2007.
Josh Harkinson	"Is Peak Oil a Waste of Energy?" *Mother Jones*, September 1, 2009. www.motherjones.com.
Robert L. Hirsch	"The Inevitable Peaking of World Oil Production," *Atlantic Council Bulletin*, vol. 16, no. 3, October 2005. www.acus.org.
Toni Johnson	"The Return of Resource Nationalism," Council on Foreign Relations, August 13, 2007. www.cfr.org.
Michael T. Klare	"Just How Addicted to Oil Are We?" *Mother Jones*, February 10, 2006. www.motherjones.com.
Joshua Kurlantzick	"Put a Tyrant in Your Tank," *Mother Jones*, vol. 33, no. 3, May–June 2008. www.motherjones.com.

Ben Levisohn   "Sizing Up the New Oil Spike,"
BusinessWeek, June 1, 2009.
www.businessweek.com.

Daniel Litvin   "Oil, Gas and Imperialism," *Guardian*
(UK), January 4, 2006.
www.guardian.co.uk.

Michael Lynch   "'Peak Oil' Is a Waste of Energy,"
New York Times, August 24, 2009.
www.nytimes.com.

David MacKay   "Let's Get Real About Alternative
Energy," CNN, May 13, 2009.
www.cnn.com.

Fred Magdoff   "The World Food Crisis: Sources and
Solutions," *Monthly Review*, vol. 60,
no. 1, May 2008.

Clifford D. May   "Oil and War Mix: Having the
Former Has Meant Winning the
Latter," *National Review Online*,
December 20, 2007.
www.nationalreview.com.

Reza Molavi and   "The International Politics of Peak
K. Luisa Gandolfo   Oil and Energy Policy,"
e-International Relations, July 28,
2009. www.e-ir.info.

Carlos Pascual   "The Geopolitics of Energy: From
Security to Survival," Brookings
Institution, January 2008.
www.brookings.edu.

Reuters	"FACTBOX–How Countries Have Coped with the Oil 'Curse,'" November 22, 2009. www.reuters.com.
Bryan Walsh	"Remembering the Lessons of the *Exxon Valdez*," *TIME*, March 24, 2009. www.time.com.
Andy Webb-Vidal	"U.S. Military Sees Oil Nationalism Spectre," *Financial Times*, June 25, 2006. www.ft.com.
Steven R. Weisman	"Oil Producers See the World and Buy It Up," *New York Times*, November 28, 2007. www.nytimes.com.

Index

A

Accountability, government, 49, 52–53, 87
See also Government corruption
Addiction to oil. See Oil dependence
Afghanistan conflict, 2001-, 45
African oil
countries' conflict, 48, 49, 50
new producers, 47, 51, 149
reserves, 32, 126, 148
Agence France-Presse (AFP), 88–91
Agriculture systems, strains, 162–169, 188
See also Crop sources, biofuels; Organic farming; Pesticides and fertilizers
Air pollution
agriculture-related, 97
carbon emissions, 68, 188–189
Chinese emissions, 89
oil history, 63, 67–68, 80, 85
Airline industry
fuels, 17, 34, 95, 138
post-9/11, 133
Alaska
oil reserves, 127
oil spills, 60–62, 67
Algeria, 48, 49
Alternative energies. See Renewable and green energy
Amazon rain forest, oil exploration and degradation, 83–85

American Recovery and Reinvestment Act (2009), 183–184, 185, 187–188
Angola, 53, 54, 150
Animals, oil spill harms, 60, 61, 67, 73, 75
Anticlines, 64
Appliances, 184
Arab-Israeli wars, 76–77, 106
Arctic National Wildlife Refuge (ANWR), 127
Authoritarian governments. See Government corruption
Automobile industry
Asia, 28, 36, 131, 132, 158–160
global recession and, 114, 130
history, 17–18
petroleum-only vehicles as problem, 28–29
production rates, 27–28, 159
U.S., 130, 187–188
Azerbaijan, 51

B

Bakken Shale (North Dakota), 127
Barter, for infrastructure improvements, 54–55
Bashir, Omar al-, 52
Batteries, 29–30, 140, 143, 159, 187
Battery-powered vehicles, 71, 131
Beef, 111, 167
Benzene, 80–81
Biden, Joe, 187
Bioaccumulation, 73–74

Biodiversity, 83
Biofuels
    agricultural production, 32, 33, 96, 97, 120, 166–167
    agricultural use, 165–166
    defined, 96, 142–143
    government support, 187
    growing, but not significantly, 119, 144
    as oil alternative, 116, 119, 132, 142–143
    pros and cons, 96–98, 119–120
Biomass fuels, 96, 98, 142–143
Birol, Fatih, 107–110
Bissell, George, 17
Bitumen. *See* Heavy oil; Oil sands
Black market oil sales, 50, 52
Blair, Tony, 53
Bolivia, 30, 50
Boycotts, conflict oil, 52
BP
    2009 *Statistical Review of World Energy*, 157
    Iraq presence, 41
    oil use and reserves statistics, 171, 172
Brammer, Marc, 155–156
Brazil
    oil supply, 23, 57, 120, 122, 125, 148
    sugar-based ethanol, 33, 122
Bright Artemis oil spill, 2006, 75
Brown, Gordon, 130, 156
Bush, George W.
    energy task forces, 46–47
    foreign/energy policy commentary, 23
    military policy, 42, 43
    oil production encouragement, 146

oil shale, 127
oil spill consequences, 62
Butler, Rhett, 83–87

C

CAFE (Corporate Average Fuel Economy) standards, 69, 158
Cambodia, 51
Cambridge Energy Research Associates, studies, 155–156, 157
Canadian oil
    sands, 29, 93, 110, 112, 119, 120–121, 134, 148
    shale, 127
Cap rock, 64
Carbon caps, 189–190
Carbon capture and storage (CCS), 39, 90, 93
Carbon dioxide
    emissions, 68, 189
    produced, non-conventional oil gleaning, 112, 120, 121
    use, oil recovery, 38
    See also Global warming
Cars. *See* Automobile industry; Driving habits; Vehicles
Carson, Rachel, 193
Cartels. *See* Monopolies
Caspian basin producers, 47, 51, 149
Castro, Fidel, 57
Cellulosic ethanol, 97–98
Chad, 51
Chávez, Hugo, 121
Chevron
    Gulf of Mexico reserves, 125
    Iraq presence, 41
China
    automobile industry, 131, 132, 158–160

imports, and infrastructure aid (Angola, Nigeria), 54

imports, and political deals (Sudan, Myanmar), 52

increasing fossil fuel demand/ use, 19, 35, 52, 88, 89–90, 117, 119, 122–123, 131, 147, 157–160

international energy policy and power, 123

oil supply, 23, 134

China National Petroleum Corporation, 23

Civil wars
  global totals and trends, 46, 51
  Iraqi factions, 43, 44–45, 49
  oil producing countries, 46, 49–51

Cleanup, oil spills
  failed/inadequate attempts, 60–61, 62, 84
  methods and needs, 74–75, 77
  rain forest difficulties, 85

Climate change. *See* Global warming

Coal
  coal-to-liquid processing, 95, 110, 119
  future demand predictions, 88, 89–90, 95, 144
  power generation, 71, 90, 95–96, 186

Cogan, James, 41–45

Collier, Paul, 53

Colombia, 49, 50

Colorado
  oil shale, 127
  pollution, 81, 82

Community-sponsored agriculture programs (CSAs), 167–168

Conflicts. *See* Civil wars; Government corruption; Iraq War, 2003-; Middle East conflicts; "Oil curse" and conflicts; Resource scarcity conflicts

Connor, Steve, 107–112

Consumption rates
  China, 35, 89, 117, 122–123, 147, 157–160
  European Union, 32
  future predictions, 27, 35, 63, 88–91, 118–119, 130–131
  global, 19, 34, 109–110, 117, 122–123
  per-person, 34, 35
  United States, 25, 32, 69, 89, 117, 122–123, 181
  See also Supply and demand

Conventional oil, 93

Corn crops, ethanol, 32, 33, 96, 97, 120, 166–167

Corporate Average Fuel Economy (CAFE) standards, 69, 158

Corruption. *See* Government corruption

Côte d'Ivoire, 51

Crop sources, biofuels, 32, 33, 96, 97, 120, 166–167

Crownover, Myra, 37–40

Crude oil processing, 66–67, 93

Cuba, 57, 169

Currency fluctuations, 48, 86–87, 115, 173, 176

D

Debts, national, 86, 101, 151

Deepwater oil and drilling, 94–95, 104, 116, 119, 122, 125, 126, 148, 153

Deforestation, 83, 97, 121

DeGette, Diana, 82

Demand. *See* Consumption rates; Supply and demand

Democratic Republic of the Congo, 50, 52

Denmark, 185

Department of Energy. *See* U.S. Department of Energy

Department of Interior. *See* U.S. Department of Interior

Depression scenarios, 100–101

    See also Recessions, global

Developing countries

    free trade and pollution, 100

    increasing fossil fuel use, 19, 35–36, 52, 88, 89–90, 122–123, 131, 140, 147, 157–160

    non-diversified oil economies, and "oil curse," 24, 46–55, 86–87

Diatoms, 170

Diesel fuels, 95, 96, 97, 162, 163–164, 165, 166, 168

Diplomatic challenges, amidst oil's power, 23–24, 51–52, 123

    See also Government corruption

Disclosure laws, 81

DNO (Norwegian oil firm), 41–42

Domestic drilling. *See* Drilling; Energy independence; Offshore drilling

Drake, Edwin L., 16–17, 21, 180

Drilling

    history and processes, 66, 180

    Western U.S. degradation, 79–82

Driving habits, 68–69, 187, 188

Dunning, Brian, 133–138

"Dutch disease," 48

    See also "Oil curse" and conflicts

E

East Timor, 47, 51

Economic progress, and fossil fuels link, 19, 21, 31–33, 108, 111, 113, 193–194

Economic recessions. *See* Recessions, global

Economic sanctions, 51, 52

Economy, global

    adaptability, 134–135, 137–138

    oil as growth business, 2009-2029, 129–132

    oil dependence, 16, 34–36, 52, 140, 172, 176

    oil will continue to have impact, 109, 144–152

    See also Investment, oil production; Recessions, global

Economy, U.S.

    American Recovery and Reinvestment Act (2009), 183–184, 185, 187–188

    clean energy-based, 180–190

    depression scenarios, 100–101

    oil and gas industry as essential, 37–40

    recessions, 92, 156

Ecosystems

    marine, 73–74, 78

    rain forest, 83

Ecuador

    national debt, 86

    rain forest areas degradation, 83–85

Egypt, 152

Electric vehicles, 71, 131, 132

Electricity
  coal-powered, 71, 90, 95–96, 186
  home use, history, 17–18
  nuclear-powered, 71, 98–99
  oil's role, 18, 21
  renewable sources, 140–141, 165–166, 171, 185, 186
  smart grid development, 131, 186
Embargoes
  OPEC, 1973, 23, 26, 70, 106
  US-Japan, 22
Emerging nations. *See* Brazil; China; Developing countries; India
Emissions. *See* Biofuels; Coal; Global warming; Vehicles
Energy efficiency, households, 183–184
Energy independence
  global security goals, 140, 175
  'independence' definitions, 25–26
  Obama goals/ideals, 24–25, 27, 181–183, 187, 188, 190
Energy Information Administration, 34, 35, 106, 116–119, 122–124
Energy security
  achievement through alternative energies, 140
  government policy points, 154, 158, 175
  necessary to sustain global economy, 170–179
Enhanced oil recovery, 38–39
Environmental Literacy Council, 31–33
Environmental Protection Agency (EPA), 80, 189

Environmental stewardship
  biofuels pros and cons, 96–98, 119–120
  chaos factor negation, 100–101
  green movement beginnings, 193
  international agreements, 27
  oil company exemptions and avoidance, 61–62, 79–82
  oil's heavy toll, 63–72
  pricing options, 71–72
  See also Animals, oil spill harms; Global warming; Non-conventional oil and sources; Oil spills; Rain forests; Sensitive land/habitat areas
Environmental Working Group, 79, 80–81
Equatorial Guinea, 50, 52
Erosion, 97
Ethanol, 32, 33, 71, 96–98, 122, 143, 166–167, 187
European Union, oil consumption, 32
Extractive Industries Transparency Initiative, 52–53
Exxon
  history, 17
  Iraq presence, 41
  oil spills, 60–62, 67, 68, 85
Exxon Valdez oil spill, 1989, 60–62, 67, 68, 85

F

Farmers. *See* Agriculture systems, strains; Organic farming
Federal environmental statutes
  cancellation scenarios, 101
  limited powers, 79–82

Fertilizers and pesticides, 34, 92, 97, 111, 136–137, 162, 163

Fires, 67–68, 85

Fishing economies
oil spill harms, 60, 61, 76, 77
whaling, 17, 65

Flex-fuel vehicles, 28–29, 71, 143

Food prices
ethanol and, 32, 120, 166–167
oil in agriculture and, 163–166, 167–169

Ford, Henry, 17, 29

Ford Motor Co., 159

Forest fires, 85

Formation processes, fossil fuels, 16, 63–64, 170

France, 130

Free trade, 100

Fuel efficiency
CAFE standards, 69, 158
China, 158–159
energy independence method (inadequate), 28
improvements, 71, 131, 158, 187
incentives and penalties, 72, 159, 188

Future predictions
"chaos factor" and scenarios, 100–101
decreasing demand, 118–119, 177
increased demand and increased environmental damages, 88–91, 95
increasing demand, 27, 63, 130–131
oil as growth business, 2009-2029, 129–132

oil price increases, 147–149, 153–161
See also Developing countries

G

Gas prices (pump)
China, 158
taxes, 72, 173
U.S., 69, 106, 135, 158
See also Oil prices (per barrel)

Gasoline, 68, 132, 163–164

Gazprom, 23, 150–151

General Motors, 159

Genetically-engineered crops, 97

Geothermal energy, 141–142

Germany
oil dependence history, 22
solar energy, 185

Global warming
degree increases, 90, 188
denials, 128
energy taxes to combat, 175
fuel extraction contributions, 112, 120, 121
Obama administration plans to combat, 188–190
oil economies contribution, 19, 32, 71, 89–90, 189
peak oil relationship, 92–93, 110, 112, 119
technology shifts required to combat, 70, 88–89, 182, 183

Gold, 136

Gore, Al, 128

Government corruption
cause of supply shortages, 56–57
oil-dependent economies, 24, 49, 50–51, 56–58, 86, 87
reductions, transparency initiatives, 52–53

Grades, oil quality, 93
Green energy sources. *See* Renewable and green energy
Green job creation, 183, 184, 185, 186
Greenhouse gases. *See* Carbon dioxide; Global warming
Greenpeace
    article: oil spills and leaks, 73–78
    article: rising oil prices may threaten production and supply, 153–161
Grinning Planet, 92–102
Groundwater contamination, 80–81, 81–82, 85
    See also Water pollution (non-oil spill)

H

Halliburton, 82
Hatch, Orrin, 127
Hathaway, Terry, 33–36
Hayward, Tony, 157
Hazardous wastes
    groundwater, 80–81, 81–82, 85
    nuclear, 98–99
Heavy oil, 93, 119, 120, 121–122
Heinberg, Richard, 113–115, 163, 169
High speed rail, 187
Hinchey, Maurice, 82
History
    industrialization, 191–193
    oil formation, 16, 63–64, 170
    oil use, 16–19, 110–111
    transportation modes, 138
Home improvement credits, 183–184
Horwitt, Dusty, 79–82

Huaoroni people (Ecuador), 83–84
Hubbert, M. King, 18, 104–105, 106, 134, 193–194
Human rights violations, oil-producing countries, 23–24
Hurricane Katrina (2005), 37
Hussain, Ali, 170–179
Hybrid vehicles, 33, 71, 95–96, 132, 187
Hydraulic fracturing, 81, 82
Hydroelectricity, 171
Hydrogen energy, 99–100, 135
Hydrogen fuel cell vehicles, 33, 71, 143

I

Immigration, 151–152
Imperialism
    historic, 22
    Iraq war as, 41–45
Incentive programs, fuel efficiency, 72, 159, 188
India
    auto industry, 28, 36
    increasing fossil fuel use, 19, 28, 35, 36, 52, 88, 89–90, 119, 131
Indian Ocean oil spills, 75
Indigenous peoples, 83–85, 85–86
Indonesia, 50
Industrial Revolution, 191–194
Infrastructure
    needs, developing oil-producing countries, 48, 54–55, 86, 87, 150, 151
    oil drilling and exploration, environmental impact, 79, 83, 84, 85

oil infrastructure sabotage, 67–68, 76–77
oil rigs, Texas, 37–38
Innovations. *See* Technology innovations
Internal combustion engine, and innovations, 16, 17, 131, 132
International Energy Agency (IEA)
   global demand predictions, 27, 88–91, 109, 130–131, 177
   Middle East oil dependence commentary, 30
   oil supply/peak oil reports, 107, 108, 109, 111–112, 121, 175
International Energy Forum, 178
International Energy Outlook (Energy Information Administration report), 116–119, 121, 122–124
International environmental treaties, 27
Investment, oil production
   continuing, 91, 172–174, 178
   declines, 27, 107–108, 115, 128, 130, 145, 147–149, 174, 175, 176
   non-traditional sources, 121–122, 160
Iowa, wind energy potential, 185
Iran
   Chinese relations, 123
   domestic gasoline policy, 57, 151
   export revenues, 145, 150, 151
   government corruption, 49, 50, 56
   oil supply and production, 23, 126, 170, 177
   U.S. diplomatic history, 22–23

Iraq
   economy, 43, 150
   military, 43–44
   oil production, 170, 172, 177
   reserves, 41, 42, 126, 172, 177
Iraq War, 2003-
   oil as reason, 41–45, 46
   oil within civil war, 49, 50
Israel, wars, 76–77, 106
Ivory Coast, 51

J

Japan
   oil dependence history, 22
   solar energy, 185
Job creation, 183, 184, 185, 186
Jordan, 152

K

Kazakhstan, 48, 51
Kim Il-Sung, 57
Klare, Michael T.
   article: oil and global economy, 144–152
   article: world oil output drops, 116–124
Korea, 159
Kurdish region, Iraq, 41–42, 44–45
Kurdistan Regional Government, 45
Kuwait
   Iraqi oil sabotage, 67–68
   oil production, 170, 177

L

Lebanon oil spills, 76–77
Life expectancy, 31
Lithium, 30

Local food systems support, 167–169

Luft, Gal, 21–30

M

Malaysian oil, 23

Maliki, Nouri al-, 43, 44

Mangrove swamps, 67, 76

Manufacturing uses of oil, 18, 21, 34, 92, 97, 111, 135, 136, 162–163, 171

Marginal oil resources. *See* Non-conventional oil and sources

Marine ecosystems, 73–74, 78

Marine life. *See* Animals, oil spill harms

Mark, Jason, 162–169

Market-based carbon caps, 189–190

Mauritania, 51

McLamb, Eric, 191–194

Meat production, 111, 167

Methane hydrates, 99

Mexican oil

declining, 121

government control and revenues, 57, 150

history, 18

Middle East conflicts, 76–77, 106, 152

Middle East oil

market control predictions, 30, 108

peak has passed, 109

political angling, 18, 22, 41, 42, 43

rejection, for energy independence, 175

reserves, 172, 177

supply increase predictions, 88, 91, 134, 177

Model T (automobile), 17, 29

Monopolies

battery materials sources, 30

OPEC as, 18, 26, 28

power structures, 25–26

Myanmar, 47, 51, 52

N

Namibia, 51

National Academy of Sciences, 105

National Iranian Oil Corporation, 23

National oil supplies, 23, 56–57, 150

Natural gas

agriculture uses, 162, 163

Dutch reserves, 48

Iraq reserves, 42

Russian revenue declines, 150, 151

U.S. production, 37, 79, 81

Netherlands, 48

New Mexico, pollution, 81–82

New technologies. *See* Technology innovations

Nigeria

infrastructure improvement, 54, 150

native tribes, exploitation, 86

struggles despite oil wealth, 48, 49, 50

Non-conventional oil and sources

economic reasons, exploration slowing/stopping, 148, 153–154, 155–157, 160

specific finds, 125–127

types described, 93, 104, 110,
112, 116, 119–122
See also Biofuels
North American reserves, 32
See also Canadian oil; Mexican oil; United States
North Dakota
land use, agriculture, 167
oil shale, 127
North Korea, 57
North Sea oil
declines, 57, 121
new discoveries, 126
Nuclear power generation, 71,
98–99, 171, 183
Nuclear waste storage, 98, 171,
183

O

Obama, Barack
energy independence ideals,
24–25, 27, 181–183, 187,
188, 190
Iraq occupation continuation,
42, 44, 45
need for U.S. clean energy
economy, 180–190
Offshore drilling
break-even point challenges,
148, 153–155
deepwater, 94–95, 116, 119,
122, 125, 126, 148, 153
Gulf of Mexico operations,
37–38, 126, 148
pros and cons, 29
U.S. debate, 37
Oil companies
American, 17, 18
contracts and risk, 54, 74–75
economic importance, 144–
152, 172

environmental care exemptions, 61–62, 79–82
environmental movement focus, 87
future decisions and challenges, 153–157, 160–161
Iraq presence, 41–42, 42–43
oil sources, transparency, 53
rain forest degradation, 83–85
See also Investment, oil production; National oil supplies; specific companies
"Oil curse" and conflicts, 24, 46–
55, 86–87
Oil dependence
American, 22–24, 41–45, 70,
105–106
global conflicts, history, 21–
22, 30
global economy, 16, 52, 140,
152, 172, 176
See also Energy independence;
Oil-dependent economies
Oil-dependent economies
political corruption potential,
24, 56–58
strife potential, decreased oil
demand, 27
Oil-for-development contracts,
54–55
Oil Pollution Act (1990), 62
Oil prices (per barrel)
agriculture costs, 162–163
"break points," 155–157
future scenarios, and chaos
factor, 100–101
global recession and, 26–27,
56, 113–114, 115, 144–147
peak oil pinpointing, 113, 128,
130
political power and, 23–24,
144–145, 149–152

rising global demand and, 19, 27, 56, 91, 119
rising prices, threats to production/supply, 108–109, 113, 149, 153–161
volatility, 49, 54, 130, 147–150, 157
See also Gas prices (pump)
Oil rushes, 17, 65
Oil sands
added environmental harms, 110, 112, 120–121
break-even analysis, 148, 153–154, 155–157, 160
as non-conventional oil source, 29, 93, 110, 112, 116, 119, 134
Oil shale, 29, 93, 116, 119, 120, 126–127
Oil spills
Alaska, 60–62
environmental harms (general), 67, 68, 73–75
inland waters, 84, 85
recent spills, details, 75–77
risks, deepwater drilling, 73, 95
OPEC. *See* Organization of the Petroleum Exporting Countries (OPEC)
Organic farming, 162–163, 165–166, 167–168
Organization of the Petroleum Exporting Countries (OPEC), 18, 26, 27
countries' wealth losses, 47
market and production declines, 70, 113, 146
market increase predictions, 91, 108
oil embargo, 23, 26, 70, 106

oil supply security, 172–174, 175–176
reserves, 172

P

Pakistan, 45
Palin, Sarah, 62
Peak demand, 131, 154–155, 157, 158
Peak oil
conventional vs. nonconventional sources, 29, 93–94, 104, 110, 112, 116, 119–122, 153–155
defined, 63, 105, 111–112, 133, 149
global (already peaked), 93–94, 113–115, 164
global (current/recent production rates), 19, 70, 107–112, 117–118
Hubbert predictions, 18, 104–106, 134, 193–194
as myth, 125–128, 162
oil executives' opinions, 157
scenario could cause environmental disasters, 92–102
U.S. production (peaked), 18, 63, 69, 104–105, 134, 194
See also Supply and demand
Pennsylvania oil, 16–17, 21, 65, 66, 129, 180–181
Personal consumption
driving habits and, 68–69, 71–72
oil, 34, 35
Pesticides and fertilizers, 97, 111, 136–137, 162, 163
Petrobras (Brazil), 23, 125
Petróleos de Venezuela, S.A., 23

Petroleum in manufacturing, 18, 21, 34, 92, 97, 111, 135, 136, 162–163, 171
Petronas (Malaysia), 23
Philippines oil spills, 76
Phosphorous, 136–137
Plastics, 18, 21, 34, 92, 135, 136, 163, 171
Plug-in hybrid vehicles, 95–96, 98, 131, 132, 187
Political corruption. *See* Government corruption
Pollution. *See* Air pollution; Oil spills; Water pollution (non-oil spill)
Population rates
    India and China, 35, 36, 133
    Industrial Revolution influence, 192–193
Public opinion
    energy independence, U.S., 24
    environmental concerns, 32–33
Putin, Vladimir, 150

Q

Quality of life
    improvements, 21, 31–33

R

Rail travel, 138, 187
Rain forests
    deforestation for biofuel crops, 97
    oil exploration and extraction, 83–85
Recessions, global
    emissions decreases following, 92

oil market effects, 26–27, 56, 130, 145–147, 154, 155, 156
oil tyranny and, 56, 58
recovery attempts, amidst peak oil, 107–108, 109, 113–115, 146–147
Reefs
    oil spill damages, 67, 76
    Texas development, 38
Refining, environmental impacts, 67
Regulations, environmental. *See* Federal environmental statutes; International environmental treaties
Renewable and green energy
    biofuels renewability, 96
    energy independence strides, 24, 39, 140, 182–183
    materials sources considerations, 29–30, 71, 140–141
    non-embracement consequences, 88–89, 145, 160–161
    oil spill eradication, 78
    percentages of all energy, 171, 185
    transition needs and attempts, 19, 32–33, 70, 131, 135–136, 140–143, 182–190
    See also Biomass fuels; Geothermal energy; Solar energy; Tidal power; Wind energy
Reparations, oil-related, 61–62, 84, 85–86
Research and Experimentation Tax Credit, 188
Reserves
    capacity assessment, 107, 108, 109, 111, 171, 172

environmental dangers, 29
Middle Eastern, 18, 22
national oil supplies, 23, 150, 151
new/nonconventional, 29, 51, 93, 104, 110, 112, 116, 119, 120–122, 125–127, 153–155
OPEC control, 18, 26
United States, 25, 69, 93, 125, 126–127, 134
See also Peak oil
Resource scarcity conflicts
energy, 21–22, 123–124, 129, 140, 149–150
food/water, 25–26, 32, 120
Rice, Condoleezza, 24
Road clearing/construction, 79, 83, 84, 85
Rockefeller, John D., 17
Roosevelt, Franklin D., 22
Ross, Michael L., 46–55
Rotary drilling, 66
Russian oil
government corruption and, 49, 56, 57
national system, 23, 57, 150–151
production drops, 57, 134
reserves, 32, 134, 150
supply increase predictions, 88, 91

S

Safe Drinking Water Act (1974), 81, 82
Salazar, John, 82
Salt, history, 25–26
Sanctions, 51, 52
São Tomé and Príncipe, 51
Sarkozy, Nicolas, 130

Saudi Arabia
International Energy Forum, 178
market increase predictions, 91
oil production and drops, 27, 146, 148, 170, 173, 176, 177
oil revenue spending, 150, 151
U.S. diplomatic history, 22, 23, 146
U.S. oil source, 70, 145, 146
Saudi Aramco, 23, 148, 173
Schwarz, Jason, 125–128
Security, energy. *See* Energy security
Seismic analysis and surveying, 65
Sensitive land/habitat areas
marine: oil spill damages, 60, 67, 76
rain forests: oil exploration, 83–87
Shell
Hubbert's geological research, mid-20th century, 18, 104–105
Nigerian oil exploits, 86
nonconventional oil desires, 110, 126
Shipping, environmental impacts, 66–69, 164
See also Oil spills; Transportation
Shortages and rationing, gasoline, 57, 106, 182
Silent Spring (Carson), 193
Silicon, 137, 140–141
Smart grid electricity, 131, 186
Smog, 68, 73
Soil issues, biofuels, 97–98
Solar energy, 71, 140–141, 165–166, 171, 185, 186

Solar I oil spill, 2006, 76

Southeast Asia, new production, 47, 51

Soy crops, biodiesel, 96, 97

Speculation, markets, 127–128, 147

Spills. *See* Oil spills

Standard Oil Company, 17

Status of Forces Agreement, Iraq (2008), 43–44

Sudan, 49, 50, 52, 123

Supertankers, 66–67

Supply and demand

coal demand, 88, 89, 95

corruption blocking supply, 56–57

current/recent production rates, 26, 27, 70, 113, 117–118, 154

increasing demand and increasing environmental damage, 88–91, 140

oil pricing effects, 19, 27, 56, 91, 119, 144–147, 149–151, 153–161

peaked demand, 131, 154–155, 157, 158

production drops, and predictions, 107–109, 112, 113–114, 116–124, 134–135, 144–149

security, and global economy, 170–179

See also Consumption rates; Peak oil

Supreme Court (United States), 189

Surveying processes, 64–65

Sustainability, as human development phase, 191–194

T

Tanker ships, 66–67

oil spills, 67, 68, 75, 76

safety design improvements, 62

sinkings, 76

Tar sands. *See* Oil sands

Tata (automobile company), 28, 36

Tax credits, energy efficiency/green energy, 184, 185, 188

Taxes

gasoline, in U.S., 69

oil consumers, 72, 173–174, 178

windfall profits tax, 39

Technology innovations

environmental needs, 70, 88–89, 131, 182–183, 184, 185–188

federal support, 184, 185, 187–188

nature of evolving markets, 134–138

Texaco, 83–84

Texas

oil discoveries, 17

oil economy, 37–40

wind energy capacity, 185

Thailand, 49

Tidal power, 142, 186

Tolls, roads, 71–72

Tourism economies, 77

Trade imbalances, 48, 86–87, 181–182

Transitions, energy economies, 19

Transparency, government, 49, 52–53

Transportation

CO_2 emissions, 68

evolution, 138
food travel, 164
main use for oil, 17, 18, 21,
    34–35, 69, 111, 132, 171
oil dependence, 29
See also Shipping, environ-
    mental impacts; Vehicles
Treaties. *See* International environ-
    mental treaties
Turkmenistan, 51

U

Ukraine, 151
Unemployment, 47, 150, 151–152
Union of Concerned Scientists,
    63–72
United Arab Emirates, 148, 151–
    152, 170, 177
United Kingdom, 130, 156, 191
United Nations
    Chinese Security Council
        power, 52
    climate change conferences,
        130
United States
    clean energy economy need,
        180–190
    domestic oil discoveries, 16–
        17, 21, 64–65, 125, 129, 180–
        181
    economy, and emissions, 92
    economy, and oil/gas industry,
        37–40
    energy/military policy, 22–23,
        24, 42, 43
    food system, 163–165, 167,
        168–169
    government predictions, world
        output, 116–124
    imports, 25, 67, 69, 70, 105–
        106

imports diversification, 46–47
    imports source information,
        53, 145
    Iraq War, 41–45
    oil consumption, 25, 32, 69,
        89, 117, 122–123, 181
    oil dependence, 22–24, 70,
        105–106, 144
    oil independence, 24–26
    oil production, 18, 37, 63, 69,
        79, 104–105, 134, 194
    reserves, 25, 69, 93, 125, 126–
        127, 134
    Western states, drilling degra-
        dation, 79–82
United States Supreme Court, 189
U.S. Bureau of Land Management,
    reports, 80–81
U.S. Department of Energy
    energy efficiency standards,
        184
    Energy Information Adminis-
        tration, 34, 35, 106, 116–119,
        122–124
    energy projections, 130, 144,
        146, 147, 149
U.S. Department of Interior, 186
Utah, 127

V

Vargas Llosa, Alvaro, 56–58
Vehicles
    China, 131, 132, 158–160
    India, 28, 36
    new technologies, 71, 131,
        132, 135, 159, 187–188
    United States, 68, 69, 72, 187–
        188
    See also Automobile industry;
        Electric vehicles; Flex-fuel
        vehicles; Fuel efficiency;

Hybrid vehicles; Hydrogen fuel cell vehicles; Plug-in hybrid vehicles
Venezuela
  government corruption, 49, 56
  nationalized oil supply, 23, 150, 151
  production drops, 57
  reserves, and heavy oil, 32, 93, 119, 120, 121–122
  U.S. oil source, 18, 70
Vietnam, 51

W

Water pollution (non-oil spill)
  agriculture-related, 97
  drilling, 73, 80–82, 85
  oil sands extraction, 121
  vehicle-related, 68, 71
  See also Oil spills
Wave power, 142, 186

West Virginia oil, 64–65
Western United States
  environmental damages, drilling, 79–82
  oil shale reserves, 93, 120, 126–127, 134
Whaling industry, 17, 65
Wind energy, 39, 71, 141, 171, 185, 186
Windfall profits tax, 39
World Energy Outlook 2006, 175
World Energy Outlook 2007, 88–91
World War II, 22
Wyoming
  oil shale, 127
  pollution, 80–81

Y

Yergin, Daniel, 129–132
Yucca Mountain nuclear waste facility, 98

DATE DUE

DEC

14 DAY LOANS
NO RENEWALS

DEMCO, INC. 38-2931